BASIC SPANISH FOR THE HEALTH PROFESSIONS

Irene Fernandez

About the Book

Basic Spanish for the Health Professions introduces basic Spanish grammar and basic vocabulary used in the medical professions. Each lesson presents vocabulary used in everyday situations by health care professionals in different work settings (hospitals, doctor's offices and emergency rooms).

The textbook also highlights a theme around Hispanic cultural topics and traditions in the medical field. The cultural notes in each lesson are broad generalizations about a heterogeneous group of Latinos. Health Care providers should look more deeply into the particular cultural, linguistic, and socioeconomic characteristics of their patient's backgrounds.

A website accompanies the textbook. The website provides additional resources such as grammar video tutorials, audio files for vocabulary and dialogs, and electronic flashcards that help the student with pronunciation and easy access to phrases used in each lesson.

https://sites.google.com/site/spanishforthehealthprofessions/

This textbook and website can be used for self-study, as materials in a traditional college course or as part of an online course.

About the Author

Irene Fernandez is currently working at North Shore Community College as a full-time Spanish professor. She has also worked at Middlesex Community College and Salem State University.

She develops and applies technology for web-based, hybrid, and distance learning courses. She developed and/or directed the development of higher levels of Spanish, as well as specialized Career Spanish courses: i.e. Spanish for Criminal Justice, Spanish for the Health Professions, Spanish for Human Services, Spanish for Teachers and Spanish for Business and Finance.

Her research activities involved the development of new approaches to teaching foreign languages in order to improve, innovate and expand the Language Program. Due to her expertise in teaching models and best practices, she was invited to participate in the Carnegie Group to study the scholarship of teaching and learning. Because of her willingness to search for new delivery methods, she was awarded many mini-grants for course development and experimental models. She was awarded the Course of Distinction by the Massachusetts Colleges Online Best Practices and is a NISOD Excellence Award recipient.

Acknowledgments

I want to thank my colleagues who have helped in different capacities to develop these introductory lessons.

Professor Hazel Piper - MCC
Rebecca Morrissey - NSCC
Lance Eaton – NSCC
Brenda A Palacios

TABLE OF CONTENTS

Appendixes

Basic Spanish for the Health Professions

Basic Spanish for the Health Professions introduces basic Spanish grammar and basic vocabulary used in the medical professions. Each lesson presents vocabulary used in everyday situations by health care professionals in different work settings (hospitals, doctor's offices and emergency rooms).

Organization

Basic Spanish for the Health Professions contains six lessons: lesson 1, lesson 2, lesson 3, lesson 4, lesson 5 and lesson 6.

Each lesson contains the following sections:

1. Grammar

2. Medical Vocabulary in the form of dialogs.
    *   A cultural theme that highlights Hispanic topics and traditions in the medical field.
    *   Exercises for practice.

3. Website:

    https://sites.google.com/site/spanishforthehealthprofessions/
    *   Grammar video tutorials
    *   Audio files for dialogs
    *   Audio files for vocabulary
    *   Interactive flashcards for dialogs and vocabulary

4. **Assessment (Blackboard)**
    Quizzes and tests developed by the instructor are in Blackboard, available only through NSCC.

Lección 1   Obteniendo información básica del paciente.

Requesting basic information from the patient

Gramática

- Cognates
- Alphabet
- Personal Pronouns
- Verb "ser"
- Numbers 0-30
- Days, months, dates

Cognates

Thanks to cognates, you already know some Spanish. Cognates are words that are similar in spelling and meaning in both languages. For example: "doctor" in English is the same as "doctor" in Spanish, "emergency" is similar in spelling to "emergencia" and it has exactly the same meaning. As you learn a new language, try to find as many cognates as you can.

Examples of cognates:

Spanish	English
idea	*idea*
mamograma	*mammogram*
hospital	*hospital*
inteligente	*intelligent*
ambulancia	*ambulance*
ginecólogo	*gynecologist*
policía	*police*
emergencia	*emergency*

There are also false cognates. For example: "embarazada" does not mean "embarrassed," it means "pregnant," "costumbre" does not mean "costume," it means "custom, tradition." These are just a few examples of false cognates.

Alphabet

English in the US varies from English spoken in England. English even varies from state to state in this country. The same way, Spanish varies depending on the country or region where it is spoken. Colloquialisms, regionalisms, idioms, accents, vocabulary are somewhat different. Even though this is true, Spanish speakers can understand each other.

In many Spanish speaking countries as well as in Spain, Spanish is called "El Castellano" (Castilian). Spanish is a phonetic language and letters have specific sounds. Once these sounds are learned, pronunciation becomes fairly easy.

Letter	Letter Name	Phonetic	Letter	Letter Name	Phonetic
a	a	*ah*	n	ene	*eneh*
b	be	*beh*	ñ	eñe	*enyeh*
c	ce	*seh*	o	o	*oh*
ch	che	*cheh*	p	pe	*peh*
d	de	*deh*	q	cu	*coo*
e	e	*eh*	r	ere o	*edeh*
f	efe	*efe*	rr	erre	*errreh*
g	ge	*heh*	s	ese	*eseh*
h	hache	*ahcheh*	t	te	*teh*
i	i	*ee*	u	u	*ooh*
j	jota	*hotah*	v	uve	*oo-bay*
k	ka	*kah*	w	uve doble	*oo-bay-dob-lay*
l	ele	*eleh*	x	equis	*ehkiss*
ll	elle	*ehyeh*	y	ye	*eegree egga*
m	eme	*emeh*	z	ceta	*setah*

11

In 2010, in an effort to unify and simplify Spanish spelling, the Royal Spanish Academy (La Real Academia de la Lengua Española) reduced the "Abecedario" (Alphabet) to only 27 letters. Their goal was to clarify some aspects of Spanish grammar.

Despite these changes, the pronunciation of the letters CH, LL and RR continue to be distinct. These are some of the most general changes.

> **B** becomes "be"
> **V** becomes "uve"
> **Y** becomes "ye" instead of "i griega"
> **W** becomes "uve doble" instead of "doble ve"

In Spanish each letter has its own unique name and sounds except for the letter H that is silent as in "Hola".

Personal Pronouns

Personal pronouns are not used as often as they are in English. Spanish speakers tend to drop the pronouns when they are used in sentences.

For example: "Soy la enfermera" instead of "**Yo** soy la enfermera" (I'm the nurse). **YO** (I) was dropped in the first sentence.

	Singular		**Plural**
yo	*I*	**nosotros/as**	*We*
tú	*You informal*	**vosotros/as**	*Plural of "tú"*
él	*He*	**ellos**	*They (masculine)*
ella	*She*	**ellas**	*They (feminine)*
usted	*You formal*	**ustedes**	*Plural of "usted"*

There are also differences in the use of the pronoun "you." "You" is translated as "tú", "usted", "vosotros" and "ustedes" but they are not interchangeable.

Tú	(You familiar) It is used with a family, friend, and someone the same age or younger.
Usted	(You formal) It is used to address someone you do not know well, someone older or an authority such as a police officer. This is abbreviated as "Ud."
Vosotros	Plural of "tú." This is used to address a group of friends. This is only used in Spain.
Ustedes	Plural of "usted." In Latin America 'ustedes' is the plural of "tú" and "usted." This is abbreviated as "Uds."

When interacting with patients, use the formal pronoun "usted" or "ustedes" to be formal and show respect.

Verb "ser"

The verb "ser" is an irregular verb; all forms are different from the infinitive form. This is the conjugation of the verb "ser". Conjugate means to put together the pronoun and the verb.

Ser (*to be*)					
Singular			**Plural**		
Yo	**soy**	*I am*	Nosotros/as	**somos**	*We are*
Tú	**eres**	*You are*	Vosotros/as	**sois**	*You are*
Él		*He is*	Ellos		*They are (m)*
Ella	**es**	*She is*	Ellas	**son**	*They are (f)*
Ud.		*You are*	Uds.		*You are*

The third person singular "él, ella, Ud." share the same form of the verb as well as the third person plural "ellos, ellas, Uds."

The verb "ser" can be used to say who you are, where you are from, what your nationality is and what you do. It describes someone or something. It is also used to tell time, dates and days of the week.

Examples:

– Soy el Dr. Rojas.	*I'm Dr. Rojas.*
– Soy de Boston.	*I'm from Boston*
– Soy americano.	*I'm American.*
– El paciente es alto.	*The patient is tall.*
– El bolígrafo es rojo.	*The pen is red.*
– Son las dos.	*It is two.*
– Es el 4 de junio.	*It is June 4th.*
– Es martes.	*It is Tuesday*
– Soy un doctor *(male)*	*I'm a doctor*
– Soy una doctora *(female)*	*I'm a doctor*
– Soy enfermero *(male)*	*I'm a nurse*
– Soy enfermera *(female)*	*I'm a nurse*
– Somos enfermeras *(plural)*	*We are nurses*

Numbers 0-30

0 cero					
1 uno	**11** once		**21** veintiuno	*veinte y uno*	
2 dos	**12** doce		**22** veintidós	*veinte y dos*	
3 tres	**13** trece		**23** veintitrés	*veinte y tres*	
4 cuatro	**14** catorce		**24** veinticuatro	*veinte y cuatro*	
5 cinco	**15** quince		**25** veinticinco	*veinte y cinco*	
6 seis	**16** dieciséis	*diez y seis*	**26** veintiséis	*veinte y seis*	
7 siete	**17** diecisiete	*diez y siete*	**27** veintisiete	*veinte y siete*	
8 ocho	**18** dieciocho	*diez y ocho*	**28** veintiocho	*veinte y ocho*	
9 nueve	**19** diecinueve	*diez y nueve*	**29** veintinueve	*veinte y nueve*	
10 diez	**20** veinte		**30** treinta		

Numbers from 16 to 19 and from 21 to 29 can be written in two different ways, but there is no preference in the use from one way to the other. After number 30, numbers in Spanish follow predictable patterns.

Spanish speakers pair numbers when giving phone numbers. For example: 781-543-2160 would be "seventy eight, fifteen, forty three, twenty one, sixty." However, they quickly learn how phone numbers are given in the USA.

To ask someone's phone number:

¿Cuál es su número de teléfono? *What is your phone number?*
781-543-2160   siete, ocho, uno, cinco, cuatro, tres, dos, uno, seis, cero.

For short:

¿Número de teléfono?
978-762-4000   *nueve, siete, ocho, siete, seis, dos, cuatro, cero, cero, cero.*

Spanish uses an upside-down question mark at the beginning of each question.

Days of the week

The week starts on Monday. Days are not capitalized; they are all masculine and are used with the articles "el, los".

Días de la semana	*Days of the week*
El lunes	*Monday*
El martes	*Tuesday*
El miércoles	*Wednesday*
El jueves	*Thursday*
El viernes	*Friday*
El sábado	*Saturday*
El domingo	*Sunday*

¿Qué día es hoy? is "What day is it today?"

Example:

¿Qué día es hoy?	*What day is it today?*
Hoy es lunes.	*Today is Monday.*
Hoy es martes.	*Today is Tuesday.*
Hoy es domingo.	*Today is Sunday.*

Months

In Spanish, months are not capitalized.

Los meses del año	Months of the year
enero	*January*
febrero	*February*
marzo	*March*
abril	*April*
mayo	*May*
junio	*June*
julio	*July*
agosto	*August*
septiembre	*September*
octubre	*October*
noviembre	*November*
diciembre	*December*

Dates

In the Spanish speaking world, dates are given in the following way:

DAY / MONTH / YEAR

Example:

Es el 12 de enero del 2040.   *It is January 12, 2040.*

Es el 24 de diciembre del 2045.   *It is December 24, 2045.*

The equivalente of "What date is it today?" is "¿Qué fecha es hoy?"

¿Qué fecha es hoy?	*What day is it today?*
Hoy es el 31 de octubre.	*Today is October 31st.*
¿Fecha de nacimiento?	*Date of birth?*
5 de julio del 2040.	*July 5, 2040.*

Use the ordinal number "primero" (first) rather than the cardinal number "uno" for the first day of the month.

¿Qué fecha es hoy?	*What day is it today?*
Hoy es el primero de octubre.	*Today is October 1st.*

How to give Addresses

The equivalent of "what is your address?" is ¿Cuál es su dirección? For short when filling out forms you ask: ¿Dirección? - *Address?*

Some basic types of streets are:

Calle	*Street*
Avenida	*Avenue*
Plaza	*Square/Plaza*
Paseo	*Drive*

The following is the format to write a street address in most Spanish speaking countries:

- Type of street – name of the street- house number
- City (Postal code)
- City, country

Example:

¿Dirección?	**Address?**
Sr. Carlos García	*Mr. Carlos García*
Calle Los Andes #30	#30 *Los Andes Street*
La Paz, Bolivia	*La Paz, Bolivia*

18

For a more complex address:

- Type of street – name of the street- building number- floor number - door number
- City (Postal code)
- Province (not necessary if the address is in a large city)
- Country

Example:

Sr. Carlos García	*Mr. Carlos García*
Calle Los Andes #30	*#30 Los Andes Street*
Edificio El Dorado, 3 piso #2	*El Dorado building, 3rd*
floor #2	
La Paz, Bolivia	*La Paz, Bolivia*

To answer the following questions in a simple way:

¿Cuál es su dirección?	*What is your address?*
¿Dirección?	*Address?*
Avenida Salem #18	*#18 Salem Avenue*
Danvers, MA 02155	*Danvers, MA 02155*

Diálogos

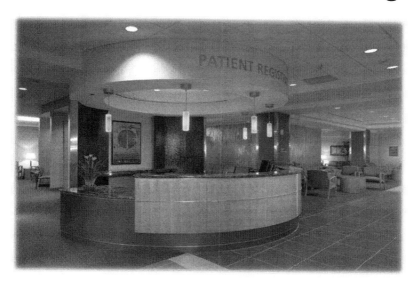

Requesting information from a patient

For translation of dialogs refer to Appendix 9.
Diálogo 1

La recepcionista llena el formulario.

Recepcionista:	Buenos días señora.
Paciente:	Buenos días Srta.
Recepcionista:	¿Nombre y apellido?
Paciente:	Ana Camacho.
Recepcionista:	¿Dirección?
Paciente:	#18 Calle Salem, Lynn MA.
Recepcionista:	¿Número de teléfono?
Paciente:	781-524-2764.
Recepcionista:	¿Fecha de nacimiento?
Paciente:	24 de diciembre (de 1977).
Recepcionista:	¿De dónde es usted?
Paciente:	(yo) Soy de Lynn.
Recepcionista:	¿Es usted soltera o casada?
Paciente:	Soy casada.

Diálogo 2

Recepcionista:	Buenos días. Pase y tome asiento por favor. ¿En qué puedo servirle?
Paciente:	Buenos días. Necesito hablar con la enfermera.
Recepcionista:	Muy bien.
Paciente:	Gracias.
Recepcionista:	De nada.

Diálogo 3

Doctor:	Buenas noches Sra. Vega. Yo soy el doctor Smith. ¿Cómo se siente?
Paciente:	No muy bien, doctor.
Doctor:	Lo siento.

Diálogo 4

Doctor:	Buenas tardes Sra. Loza.
Paciente:	Buenas tardes doctor.
Doctor:	¿Cómo está?
Paciente:	Muy mal.
Doctor:	¡Lo siento! Sólo hablo un poco de español. Necesito llamar a un intérprete.

Vocabulario

Buenos días.	*Good morning.*
Buenas tardes.	*Good afternoon.*
Buenas noches.	*Good evening.*
Hasta luego.	*See you later.*
Hasta mañana.	*See you tomorrow.*
Tome asiento.	*Have a seat.*
Lo siento.	*I'm sorry.*
Pase.	*Come in.*
Por favor.	*Please.*
Gracias.	*Thank you.*
De nada.	*You're welcome.*
Adiós.	*Bye.*
El doctor/El médico	*Male doctor*
La doctora/la médica	*Female doctor*
El enfermero/La enfermera	*Male Nurse/Female Nurse*
La recepcionista	*Receptionist*
El señor (Sr.)	*Mr.*
La señora (Sra.)	*Mrs.*
La señorita (Srta.)	*Miss*
El paciente	*Male Patient*
La paciente	*Female patient*
Pero	*but*
Escriba aquí por favor.	*Write here please.*
Despacio por favor.	*Slowly please.*
Hablo un poco de español.	*I speak a little Spanish.*

(Yo) soy el doctor.   *I'm the doctor.*

Necesito hablar con el doctor.
I need to speak with the doctor.

Necesito llamar a un intérprete.
I need to call an interpreter.

Preguntas

¿Cómo está usted?	*How are you?*
¿Y usted?	*And you?*
¿Nombre y apellido?	*Name and last name?*
¿Dirección?	*Address?*
¿Número de teléfono?	*Phone number?*
¿Fecha de nacimiento?	*Date of birth?*
¿En qué puedo servirle?	*How can I help you?*

¿Cómo se siente?   *How are you feeling?*

    Bien/Muy bien.   *Well/Very well.*

    Regular/más o menos.   *Not very well.*

    Fatal/Mal/Muy mal.   *Very bad, awful.*

¿De dónde es Ud.?   *Where are you from?*

    Soy de...   *I'm from...*

¿Es usted casado o soltero?   *Are you married or single?*

    Soy soltero/a.   *I'm single.*

    Soy casado/a.   *I'm married.*

    Soy divorciado/a.   *I'm divorced.*

    Soy viudo/a.   *I'm widow/widower.*

Práctica

1. Find 10 cognates in the dialogs and list them below. Cognates are words with similar meaning and spelling in English and Spanish.

   a. _____

   b. _____

   c. _____

   d. _____

   e. _____

   f. _____

   g. _____

   h. _____

   i. _____

   j. _____

2. What pronouns would you use in the following exercise?

   a. You point to yourself *"I"*

   b. You are talking to a patient *"you"*

   c. You are talking to your best friend *"you"*

   d. You are at a conference talking to a group of people *"you"*

   e. You refer to Maria and Ana as *"they"*

   f. You refer to Luis and Juan as *"they"*

   g. Your mother refers to herself and her sister as *"we"*

h. Your father refers to himself and his brother as *"we"*

i. You refer to Mr. and Mrs. Santos as *"they"*

j. The nurse refers to the patients as *"they"*

k. The patient refers to the nurse as *"she"*

3. Conjugate the verb "ser."

   a. Yo _____

   b. Tú_____

   c. El, ella, Ud. _____

   d. Nosotros_____

   e. Vosotros_____

   f. Ellos, ellas, Uds. _____

4. Match the following questions with the correct answers.

   a. Buenas tardes.   _____Adios.

   b. ¿Nombre y apellido por favor? _____Ana Delgado.

   c. ¿Dirección?   _____Calle Salem #18.

   d. ¿Número de teléfono?   _____Hoy es lunes.

   e. ¿Qué fecha es hoy?   _____Buenas tardes.

   f. ¿Qué día es hoy?   _____Muy mal doctor.

   g. ¿Cómo se siente?   _____Cuatro de agosto.

   h. Hasta luego.   _____dos, ocho, uno,
                                            tres, cero, uno.

5. Complete the following sentences with the verb "ser."

   a. Yo _____ el doctor.

   b. El paciente _____ de Guatemala.

   c. ¿_____ usted el doctor?

   d. Nosotros _____ las enfermeras.

   e. ¿Qué fecha _____ hoy?

   f. ¿Qué día _____ hoy?

   g. Ustedes _____ casados?

   h. Los pacientes _____ de China.

6. Reply to the following:

   a. Buenos días.

   b. ¿En qué puedo servirle?

   c. ¿Nombre y apellido por favor?

   d. ¿Dirección?

   e. ¿Número de teléfono?

   f. ¿Cómo se siente?

   g. ¿Es Ud. soltero/a o casado/a?

   h. ¿Qué fecha es hoy?

   i. ¿Qué día es hoy?

   j. Hasta luego.

7. Read the situations below and tell the patient to talk to one of the specialists. Use the vocabulary in the chart:

Especialistas	Specialists
el/la cardiólogo/a	Cardiologist
el/la oftalmólogo	Ophthalmologist
el/la ginecólogo/a	Gynecologist
el/la pediatra	Pediatrician
el/la dentista	Dentist
el/la anestesiólogo/a	Anesthesiologist
el/la urólogo/a	Urologist
el/la ortopeda	Orthopedist
el/la internista	Internist
el/la cirujano/a	Surgeon

Use the phrase: Usted necesita hablar con… *You need to speak with…*

> Modelo: *The patient has an eye infection.*
> **Usted necesita hablar con** *el oftalmólogo.*

a. The patient had a heart attack.

_____

b. The patient is pregnant.

_____

c. The patient has a urinary tract infection (UTI).

_____

d. The father of an eight year old patient.

_____

Más práctica

1. Spell your name in Spanish.

_____

2. What would you say in the following situations?

    a. You are the receptionist; greet a patient in the morning.

    b. Ask the patient: *How can I help you?*

    c. A patient is at the door, ask the patient to come in and have a seat.

    d. Ask the patient what his name and last name is.

    e. Ask for his address.

    f. Ask for his phone number.

    g. Ask your female patient if she is single or married.

    h. Ask the patient to slow down.

    i. Say goodbye to a patient that you will see tomorrow.

    j. Greet the receptionist in the afternoon and tell her that you need to speak with the gynecologist.

    k. Tell the receptionist that you need to speak with the pediatrician.

    l. Tell the receptionist that you live on 20 Salem Street.

    m. Tell the receptionist that your appointment is on January 16th.

Llene la planilla con su información.

INFORMACION DEL PACIENTE

Nombre	Primero	Segundo	Apellido

Fecha de Nacimiento   Sexo   F ☐   M ☐

Seguro Social #

Domicilio

Ciudad   Estado   Código Postal

Teléfono Hogar   Mensaje

Empleador

Estado Civil   Casado/a ☐   Soltero/a ☐   Separado/a ☐
                      Divorciado/a ☐   Viudo/a ☐

Ingreso $ Semanal ☐   Mensual ☐   Anual ☐
Número de Familiares en el Hogar____

Empleado   Sí ☐   No ☐   Es Temporal ☐

Contacto de Emergencia # de Teléfono

Tipo de seguro   Medicare   ☐ Seguro Médico   ☐
                        Ningún   ☐ Otro _____

Favor de darle su tarjeta de seguro a la recepcionista para que le tome copia.

Yo certifico que la información contenida en esta forma es correcta.

Firma de Paciente_____ Fecha _____

Firma de Individuo Responsable_____ Fecha _____

(Padre, Madre, Guardián, Esposo, Esposa)

Testigo_____ Fecha _____

Nombre del paciente: _____ # Registro Médico _____

Fill out the following form with your information.

PATIENT INFORMATION
Name: First   Middle   Last
Date of Birth   Sex   F ☐   M ☐
Social Security # Address
City   State   Zip
Home Phone   Message
Employer Name
Marital Status   Married ☐   Single ☐   Separated ☐ Divorced ☐   Widowed ☐
Income $ Week ☐   Month ☐   Year ☐   Family Size ___
Employed   Yes ☐   No ☐   Seasonal ☐
Emergency Contact Phone #
Insurance Coverage   ☐ Medicare   ☐ Private Ins. ☐ None   ☐ Other _____
Please provide receptionist with a copy of your Insurance ID card
I certify that the information contained on this form is correct to the best of my knowledge. Patients Signature _____ Date _____ Responsible Party's Signature Date_____ Date _____ Witness _____Fecha _____ Patient Name: _____ Medical Record # _____

Notas Culturales

The Hispanic patient

Hispanic patients and healthcare providers' interactions should always be cordial, formal, and respectful. A firm handshake and direct eye contact which is not too prolonged are customary. Patients will be unlikely to return if there is a lack of these components. Hispanic patients rarely disagree openly; instead they become silent and noncompliant. A good relationship based on trust and respect between Hispanic patients and healthcare providers is important to provide quality care.

LESSON 2 Un examen físico. ¿Qué partes del cuerpo le duelen? ¿Cuánto le duelen?

A physical exam. Which body parts hurt? How much do they hurt?

Gramática

- Verb "tener"
- Verb "doler"
- Gender and number of nouns
- Definite articles and indefinite articles
- Possessive adjectives
- Numbers 31-100
- Time

Verb "tener"

The verb "tener" is an irregular verb with changes in its stem. Irregular verbs do not follow patterns, they must be memorized.

TENER (*to have*)			
Singular		**Plural**	
Yo **tengo**	*I have*	nosotros/as **tenemos**	*We have*
Tú **tienes**	*You have (fam)*	vosotros/as **teneis**	*You have*
él	*He has*	Ellos	*They have (m)*
ella **tiene**	*She has*	Ellas **tienen**	*They have (f)*
Ud.	*You have (formal)*	Uds.	*You have (plural)*

The third person singular él, ella, Ud. share the same form of the verb as well as the third person plural ellos, ellas, Uds.
Examples:

Yo tengo dolor de cabeza.	*I have a headache.*
Yo tengo el libro de español.	*I have the Spanish book.*
Ellas tienen el formulario.	*They have the form.*

Verb "doler"

The verb "doler" means "to cause pain," "to hurt, to ache." This is a two-word verb. The verb "doler" does not use the pronouns "yo, tú, él, ella, usted, nosotros, vosotros or ellos" it uses the indirect object pronouns (me, te, le, nos, os, les) and has two endings. The singular form ends in "e" and the plural form ends in "en."

Singular form	Plural form
Me duele	Me duelen
Te duele	Te duelen
Le duele	Le duelen
Nos duele	Nos duelen
Os duele	Os duelen
Les duele	Les duelen

The equivalent of "My head hurts" is "Me duele la cabeza" or "La cabeza me duele." In this case the singular form of the verb "me duele" is used.

Singular

Me duel<u>e</u> la cabeza.	*My head hurts.*
Te duel<u>e</u> la cabeza.	*Your head hurts.*
Le duel<u>e</u> la cabeza.	*His/her head hurts, your head hurts.*
Nos duel<u>e</u> la cabeza.	*Our heads hurt.*
Les duel<u>e</u> la cabeza.	*Their head hurts, your head hurts.*

If what hurts is plural, for example your feet (pies), use the plural verb form.

Plural

Me duel<u>en</u> los pies.	*My feet hurt.*
Te duel<u>en</u> los pies.	*Your feet hurt.*
Le duel<u>en</u> los pies.	*Her/his feet hurt, your feet hurt.*
Nos duel<u>en</u> los pies.	*Our feet hurt.*
Les duel<u>en</u> los pies.	*Their feet hurt /your feet hurt.*

To clarify the third person singular and plural add the preposition "**a**" and the name of the person:

<u>A María</u> **le duele** la cabeza.	*María's head hurts.*
<u>A Pedro</u> **le duele** la cabeza.	*Pedro's head hurts.*
<u>A usted</u> **le duele** la cabeza.	*Your head hurts (formal).*
<u>A María y a Pedro</u> **les duele** la cabeza.	*María and Pedro's heads hurt.*
<u>A ustedes</u> **les duele** la cabeza.	*Your heads hurts (plural formal).*

The equivalent to "Where does it hurt?" is "¿Dónde <u>le duele</u>?"

¿Dónde <u>le duele</u>?	***Where does it hurt?***
Me duele la cabeza.	*My head hurts.*

"Does your head hurt?" is equivalent to "¿<u>Le duele</u> *la cabeza*?"

Sí, me duele la cabeza.	*Yes, my head hurts.*
No, no me duele la cabeza.	*No, my head doesn't hurt.*

When talking *about* patients:

<u>Al paciente</u> le duele la cabeza. *(male patient)*
<u>A la paciente</u> le duele la cabeza. *(female patient)*
The patient's head hurts.

Use of verbs

Verbs have different endings to show the person who performs the action. The verb "necesitar" (to need) ends in "o" for "yo" (I).

Yo necesit<u>o</u>   *I need*

The verb "necesitar" ends in "a" for "usted" (you).

Usted necesit<u>a</u>   *You need*

The verb "necesitar" can be followed by a second verb such as "firmar" (to sign) or "llenar" (to fill out). When this happens the first verb "necesitar" is conjugated, the second verb stays in the infinitive form without any ending.

Usted necesita <u>firmar</u> el formulario.
You need <u>to sign</u> the form.

Usted necesita <u>llenar</u> el formulario .
You need <u>to fill out</u> the form.

Gender and number of nouns

Spanish nouns can be feminine or masculine. Nouns are feminine when they end in "a," "ción," "sión," "tad" or "dad." They are masculine when they end in "o" or "ma." However, there are some exceptions.

Feminine		Masculine	
Enfermer**a**	*female nurse*	Enfermer**o**	*male nurse*
Opera**ción**	*operation*	Progra**ma**	*program*
Televi**sión**	*television*		
Probabili**dad**	*probability*		
Liber**tad**	*liberty*		
Exceptions: Mano *(hand)*		**Exceptions:** Día, Mapa *(day, map)*	

Definite articles

The article "the" in English has four different translations in Spanish: el, la, los, las.

Definite Articles			
El doctor	*The doctor*	**Los** doctores	*The doctors*
La doctora	*The (female) doctor*	**Las** doctoras	*The (female) doctors*

Indefinite articles

The articles "a" or "an' correspond to "un" or "una." The article "some" corresponds to "unos" and "unas."

Indefinite Articles			
Un doctor	*A doctor*	**Unos** doctores	*Some doctors*
Una doctora	*A (female) doctor*	**Unas** doctoras	*Some (female) doctors*

Number of nouns

Making nouns plural in Spanish is not difficult if you follow three simple rules.

1. If a noun ends in a vowel, add "s."

Estudiant**e**	estudiant**es**
Enferm**o**	enferm**os**
Enfermer**a**	enfermer**as**
Doctor**a**	doctor**as**

2. If a noun ends in a consonant, add "es."

Doctor	doctor**es**
Profesor	profesor**es**

3. For nouns ending in a "z," change the z into a 'c' and then add 'es.'

Lapiz	lápi**ces**
Feliz	feli**ces**

Possessive adjectives

Possessive adjectives help to explain to whom something belongs.

The possessive adjectives "mi, mis, tu, tus, su, sus" agree in number (singular or plural) with the nouns they modify. "Nuestro, nuestra, nuestros, nuestras" agree in gender (feminine, masculine) and number.

mi, mis	*my*
tu, tus	*your*
su, sus	*its, his, her, your, their*
nuestro/a, nuestros/as	*our*
vuestro/a, vuestros/as	*your (used only in Spain)*

The singular form "mi" is used with "libro."

   (Yo) tengo **mi** libro.   *I have my book.*

The plural form "mis" is used with "libros."

   (Yo) tengo **mis** libros.   *I have my books.*

Don't confuse "tu" meaning "your" with "tú" meaning "you informal" (personal pronoun). You informal has an accent.

   Necesito tu libro.   *I need your book.*
   Tú necesitas tu libro.   *You need your book.*

The possessive adjectives "su" and "sus" can be ambiguous. **"Su libro"** can be translated as:

   Her book
   His book
   Your book
   Their book

The possessive adjectives' meaning is usually clear by its use in the sentence. However, the preposition **"de"** along with **a pronoun** or **noun** can be used to clarify its meaning:

El libro **de** ella.　　　*Her book.*

(This translates literally as "the book of her")

El libro **de** él.　　　*His book.*
El libro **de** usted.　　*Your book.*
El libro de ellos/ellas.　*Their book.*

The possessive adjective "nuestra, nuestro, nuestras, nuestros" should agree in gender and number with the noun.

Nosotros tenemos	nuestro libro	*our book*
We have	nuestra familia	*our family*
	nuestros libros	*our books*
	nuestras familias	*our families*

Numbers 31-100

30 Treinta		**70** Setenta	
40 Cuarenta		**80** Ochenta	
50 Cincuenta		**90** Noventa	
60 Sesenta		**100** Cien	

Numbers are formed with the tens followed by the conjunction 'y' and a number.

Example:

31 treinta y uno	**40** cuarenta y uno
32 treinta y dos	**45** cuarenta y cinco
33 treinta y tres	**51** cincuenta y uno
34 treinta y cuatro	**56** cincuenta y seis
35 treinta y cinco	**67** sesenta y siete
36 treinta y seis	**72** setenta y dos
37 treinta y siete	**77** setenta y siete
38 treinta y ocho	**83** ochenta y tres
39 treinta y nueve	**95** noventa y cinco
40 cuarenta	**98** noventa y ocho

Once you master the basic pattern, you can construct any number. Example:

55 = 50 + 5   cincuenta y cinco

86 = 80 + 6   ochenta y seis

Telling Time

Spanish uses the verb "ser" for telling time. The singular form "es" is used for one o'clock and the plural form "son," for other times. Minutes can be stated by separating them from the hour using "y" (and) or "menos" (minus.)

The equivalente of "What time is it?" is "¿Qué hora es?"

For one o'clock 'uno' changes into 'una'.

1:00 Es la una.	*It is one.*
2:00 Son las dos.	*It is two.*
2:10 Son las dos y diez.	*It is ten minutes past two.*

To indicate the quarter hours use "cuarto" or "quince."

    1:15   Es la una y cuarto/quince.   *It is one fifteen.*
    2:15   Son las dos y cuarto/quince.   *It is fifteen minutes past two.*

To indicate the half hour, use "media" or "treinta".

    2:30   Son las dos y media/treinta.   *It is two thirty.*
    3:30   Son las tres y media.   *It is three thirty.*
    4:30   Son las cuatro y treinta.   *It is four thirty.*

After the half hour, Spanish uses "menos"

    2:35   Son las tres menos veinticinco.
           It is twenty- five minutes to three.

    2:40   Son las tres menos veinte.
           It is twenty minutes to three.

    2:45   Son las tres menos cuarto/quince.
           It is a quarter to three

The equivalent to "It's midnight" is "Es la medianoche" and "It's noon" is "Es el mediodía"

To ask what time a specific event is "¿A qué hora es la cita?" *What time is the appointment?*

A short way to answer this question is using "A las..." (At...)

Example:

    ¿A qué hora es la cita de la Sra. Pérez?
    What time is Mrs. Perez appointment?

    1:00   A la una.
    2:00   A las dos.
    2:10   A las dos y diez.

Time can be followed by these expressions: **de la mañana** *(in the morning)*, **de la tarde** *(in the afternoon)*, **de la noche** (in the evening).

Example:

¿Qué hora es?   *What time is it?*
Son las dos de la tarde.   *It is two in the afternoon.*

¿A qué hora es la cita de la Sra. Pérez?
What time is Mrs. Perez's appointment?

2:00 PM   A las dos de la tarde.
                 At two in the afternoon.

¿A qué hora es la cita del Sr. Poma?
What time is Mr. Poma's appointment?

2: 30 PM   A las dos de la tarde y media.
                 At two thirty in the afternoon.

Diálogos

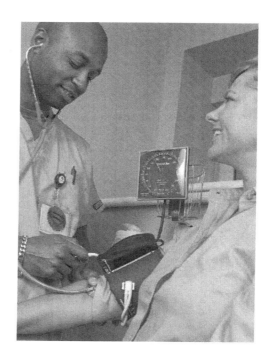

A physical exam. Which body parts hurt? How much do they hurt?

For translation of dialogs refer to Appendix 9.
Diálogo 1

Recepcionista:	Buenos días. ¿En qué puedo servirle?
Paciente:	Buenos días. Tengo un examen físico con la doctora Polo.
Recepcionista:	Muy bien ¿Nombre y apellido? Por favor.
Paciente:	(Soy) Elena Gómez.
Recepcionista:	¿Ud. tiene su tarjeta de seguro médico? Necesito una fotocopia.
Paciente:	Aquí esta.
Recepcionista:	Ud. necesita llenar el formulario.

Diálogo 2

Recepcionista:	Buenas tardes. ¿En qué puedo servirle?
Paciente:	Buenas tardes. Tengo una cita con el Dr. Ramos.
Recepcionista:	¿Nombre y apellido? por favor.
Paciente:	Elena Gómez.
Recepcionista:	Necesito su tarjeta de seguro médico.
Paciente:	No tengo seguro médico.
Recepcionista:	¿Usted paga la cuenta?
Paciente:	Si, yo pago la cuenta.

Diálogo 3

Doctor:	Ud. tiene un examen físico general hoy. ¿Cómo se siente Sra. Vera?
Paciente:	Muy bien doctor.
Doctor:	Ud. necesita un papanicolaou y un mamograma. También necesita un análisis de sangre y de orina. ¿Todavía tiene dolores de cabeza?
Paciente:	Si, tengo migrañas.
Doctor:	Aquí está la receta para las migrañas.
Paciente:	Gracias.

Diálogo 4

Doctor:	¿Cómo se siente Sra. Vargas?
Paciente:	Tengo dolores de cabeza doctor.
Doctor:	¿Le duelen sus ojos?
Paciente:	Sí, me duelen mucho mis ojos.
Doctor:	¿Le duele el cuello?
Paciente:	No, no me duele el cuello.
Doctor:	¿Tiene ruido en los oídos?
Paciente:	Si doctor, tengo ruido en los oídos.
Doctor:	¿Tiene dificultad para respirar?
Paciente:	No tengo dificultad para respirar.
Doctor:	¿Tiene tos?
Paciente:	No tengo tos.

Vocabulario

Refer to appendix 1-8 for a list of body parts.

Aquí está la receta.	*Here is the prescription.*
¿Le duelen sus ojos?	*Do your eyes hurt?*
Me duele mucho el pecho.	*My chest hurts very much.*
¿Usted paga la cuenta?	*Do (will) you pay the bill?*
Yo pago...	*I (will) pay...*
Todavía	*Still, yet*
Tengo un examen físico.	*I have a physical examination/ I have a general check up.*
Tengo dolores de cabeza.	*I have headaches.*
Tengo tos.	*I have a cough.*
Tengo ruido en mis oídos.	*I hear noise in my ears.*
Tengo dificultad para respirar.	*I have difficulty breathing.*
Formulario/planilla/forma	*form*

Necesito su planilla.
I need your form.

Necesita llenar la forma.
You need to fill out the form.

(Yo) necesito la tarjeta de seguro médico.
I need the medical insurance card.

Verbos

Pagar	*To pay*
Llenar	*To fill out*
Fumar	*To smoke*

Necesitar	*To need*
Firmar	*To sign*

Usted necesita…	***You need…***
un papanicolau.	*a pap smear.*
una radiografía.	*an X-ray.*
un electrocardiograma.	*an EKG.*
un examen físico.	*a physical examination.*
un examen general.	*a general check up.*
una mamografía .	*a mammography.*
un mamograma.	*a mammogram.*

Usted necesita …	***You need…***
un análisis de sangre.	*a blood test.*
un análisis de orina.	*a urine test.*
un análisis de material fecal.	*a stool test.*
un análisis de heces fecales.	*a stool test.*

TENER and the noun "Dolor" (pain)

¿Tiene dolor de cabeza?	*Do you have a headache?*
Sí, (yo) tengo dolor de cabeza.	*Yes, I have a headache.*
Tengo dolor de espalda.	*I have a backache.*
Tengo migrañas.	*I have migraines.*
¿Tiene dolor de estómago?	*Do you have a stomach ache?*

No, (yo) no tengo dolor de estómago.
No, I don't have a stomach ache.

"Doler" as a verb (to hurt)

¿Dónde le duele?	*Where does it hurt?*
¿Le duele el brazo?	*Does your arm hurt?*
¿Le duele el codo?	*Does your elbow hurt?*
¿Le duelen las piernas?	*Do your legs hurt?*
Me duele la cabeza.	*My head hurts.*
Me duele el estómago.	*My stomach hurts.*
Me duele la rodilla.	*My knee hurts.*
Me duelen las piernas.	*My legs hurt.*
Me duelen los brazos.	*My arms hurt.*
Me duelen mis pies.	*My feet hurt.*

Use the expressions "**mucho**" (a lot), "**un poco**" (a little), "**a veces**" (sometimes) and "**todos los días**" (every day) to make emphasis in your sentences:

Me duele <u>mucho</u> la cabeza.
My head hurts <u>a lot</u>.

Me duele <u>un poco</u> la cabeza.
My head hurts <u>a little</u>.

<u>A veces</u> me duele la cabeza.
<u>Sometimes</u> my head hurts.

Me duele la cabeza <u>todos los días.</u>
My head hurts <u>every day</u>.

Práctica

1. Find 10 cognates in the dialogs and vocabulary and list them below.

a. _____

b. _____

c. _____

d. _____

e. _____

f. _____

g. _____

h. _____

i. _____

j. _____

2. Study Appendix 1, label the picture and match the body parts.

a) la cabeza   _____mouth

b) la oreja   _____nose

c) la mejilla   _____ chin

d) la nariz   _____ neck

e) la boca   _____head

f) el mentón   _____ cheek

g) el cuello   _____ear

h) los ojos   _____ forehead

i) la frente   _____eyes

j) la garganta   _____throat

3. Study Appendix 2, label the picture and match the following body parts.

a. los hombros   _____elbow

b. el codo   _____fingers

c. la muñeca   _____arms

d. las manos   _____chest

e. los brazos   _____hands

f. los dedos de la mano _____shoulders

4. Study Appendix 3, 4 and 5 and match the following body parts.

a. la cadera   _____legs

b. la cintura   _____ankles

c. las piernas   _____feet

d. las rodillas   _____thighs

e. los tobillos   _____waist

f. los muslos   _____buttocks

g. los pies   _____knees

h. las nalgas   _____hip

50

3. What body part do you use to do the following?

    a. Smell   _____Las piernas

    b. Sing   _____Las manos

    c. Listen   _____La cabeza

    d. Run   _____La naríz

    e. Hold a book   _____La oreja

    f. See   _____Los pies

    g. Put a hat on   _____Los ojos

    h. Put shoes on   _____La boca

4. Complete the following sentences with the verb "tener."

    a. Yo _____ dolor de garganta.

    b. El Sr. y la Sra. Vargas _____dolor de

       espalda.

    c. La paciente _____dolor de pies.

    d. El doctor _____muchos pacientes.

5. Fill out the blank spaces with the indefinite article.

    a. Usted necesita _____análisis de material fecal/
                                 heces fecales.

    b. La paciente necesita _____mamografía.

    c. El paciente necesita _____examen físico.

d. Usted necesita _____análisis de orina.

e. Carlos necesita _____radiografía.

f. Usted necesita _____electrocardiograma.

g. Ana necesita _____papanicolau.

h. Yo necesito _____análisis de sangre.

6. Match the following phrases and questions using the correct form of the verb "doler."

a. Me duele la   _____Me

b. Me duele el   _____Le

c. Me duelen los   _____Piernas

d. Me duelen las   _____Cuello

e. ¿Dónde _____duele?   _____Mano

f. __duele el pecho.   _____pies

7. Use the possessive adjectives to complete the following sentences.

a. Necesito _____tarjeta de seguro médico. (her)

b. Le duelen _____brazos. (his)

c. _____cita es a las dos en punto. (our)

d. Me duelen _____piernas. (my)

8. Write the definite article for the following nouns.

    a. _____hombros

    b. _____manos

    c. _____brazos

    d. _____nariz

    e. _____pecho

    f. _____rodillas

    g. _____tobillos

    h. _____pies

    i. _____oreja

    j. _____piernas

    k. _____garganta

    l. _____espalda

9. What time do the following patients have an appointment? Answer the questions with the time provided.

Modelo: *¿A qué hora es la cita de la Srta. Suarez?*
            8:00   A las ocho.

    a. ¿A qué hora es la cita de la Sra. Vera?

        10:00   _____

b.   ¿A qué hora es la cita de la Srta. Pérez?

10:10_____

c.   ¿A qué hora es la cita del Sr. Paz?

12:00_____

d.   ¿A qué hora es la cita de la Sra. Gonzales?

12:15_____

e.   ¿A qué hora es la cita del Sr. Cortez?

1:00_____

f.   ¿A qué hora es la cita de la Sra. Vargas?

3:30_____

g.   ¿A qué hora es la cita de la Sra. Mujica?

4:40_____

h.   ¿A qué hora es la cita de la Sra. Vera?

5:55_____

i.   ¿A qué hora es la cita de la Sra. Vera?

8:30_____

What would you say in the following situations?

Recepcionista:

a. Greet the patient in the afternoon and ask "How may I help you?

b. Tell the patient that you need his/her medical insurance card.

c. Ask the patient if he/she pays the bill.

Doctor:

d. Greet the patient in the morning. Tell your female patient that you need her medical insurance card.

e. Ask your female patient how she feels and if her stomach hurts.

f. Tell your female patient that she needs a pap smear and a mammogram.

g. Tell your male patient that he needs a blood test and an EKG.

Patient

h. Tell the nurse that you have a physical examination today.

i. Tell the doctor who you are and explain your symptoms, say that your chest hurts.

j. Using the verb *tener*, tell the doctor that your head hurts.

k. Tell the receptionist that you have a physical examination.

l. Tell the nurse that your arms hurt.

10. Write four sentences describing what part of your body hurts. Use the verb "doler."

Choose a single body part for the following two sentences.

1.

2.

Use the verb *doler* in the plural form in the following two sentences.

3.

4.

11. REPORTE. Based on the following dialog, make a brief summary of the patient' symptoms.

Diálogo 4

Doctor:	¿Cómo se siente Sra. Vargas?
Paciente:	Tengo dolor de cabeza doctor.
Doctor:	¿Le duelen sus ojos?
Paciente:	Sí, me duelen mucho mis ojos.
Doctor:	¿Tiene dolor en el cuello?
Paciente:	No, no tengo dolor en el cuello.
Doctor:	¿Tiene ruidos en los oídos?
Paciente:	Si doctor.
Doctor:	¿Tiene dificultad para respirar?
Paciente:	No tengo dificultad para respirar.
Doctor:	¿Tiene tos?
Paciente:	No tengo tos.

You can start your answer with this introductory sentence: *La Sra. Vargas tiene dolor de cabeza...*

Cultural Notes

Patient's family

It is common for Hispanic patients to bring family members along to appointments and openly discuss private matters with the health care providers. Family members and friends are typically involved in a patient's health care and many times offer to act as an interpreter. However, it is preferred to have a Spanish-speaking interpreter of the same gender and preferably not related to the patient. Hispanics value 'family' over individual needs. Health care providers usually do not understand that family involvement in health care is common for Hispanic families and that this practice should be encouraged, respected and accepted.

LESSON 3 Una cita con el médico de cabecera.

An appointment with the primary care physician.

Gramática

- Regular AR, ER and IR verbs
- Conjugation of verbs
- Question words
- Verb "estar"
- Descriptive Adjectives

Regular AR, ER and IR verbs

Verbs are words that express an action or a state of being. Below is a basic list of verbs in the infinitive form. Refer to Appendix 10 for a more complete list of verbs and appendix 11 for examples of conjugation.

There are three groups of regular verbs:

1. Verbs that end in **AR**

Bus**car**	*to look for*
Camin**ar**	*to walk*
Cen**ar**	*to have dinner*
Dese**ar**	*to wish/to want*
Firm**ar**	*to sign*
Habl**ar**	*to speak*
Lleg**ar**	*to arrive*
Regres**ar**	*to return*
Trabaj**ar**	*to work*
Vacun**ar**	*to vaccinate*

2. Verbs that end in **ER**

Aprend**er**	*to learn*
Beb**er**	*to drink*
Com**er**	*to eat*
Deb**er**	*owe/should/must*
Le**er**	*to read*
Tos**er**	*to cough*
Vend**er**	*to sell*

3. Verbs that end in **IR**

Abr**ir**	*to open*
Escrib**ir**	*to write*
Sufr**ir**	*to suffer*
Viv**ir**	*to live*

Spanish verbs consist of a stem and an ending.

Examples:

Verb	stem	ending
Necesitar *(to need)*	necesit	**ar**
Beber *(to drink)*	beb	**er**
Vivir *(to live)*	viv	**ir**

Conjugation of verbs

Verbs in the infinitive form are altered from the base form when they are conjugated. Regular verbs maintain the stem and only change on the endings.

Example:

	Necesitar (to need)	Beber (to drink)	Abrir (to open)
yo	necesit**o**	beb**o**	abr**o**
tú	necesit**as**	beb**es**	abr**es**
él, ella, Ud.	necesit**a**	beb**e**	abr**e**
nosotros	necesit**amos**	beb**emos**	abr**imos**
vosotros	necesit**áis**	beb**éis**	abr**ís**
ellos, ellas, Uds.	necesit**an**	beb**en**	abr**en**

Notice that the ER and IR ending verbs are exactly the same except in the "nosotros" and "vosotros" form.

When verbs are followed by other verbs, the first one is conjugated and the second one stays the same.

Example:

Nosotros necesit<u>amos</u> **hacer** una cita.   *(Second verb "hacer")*
*We <u>need</u> to **make** an appointment.*

El paciente deb<u>e</u> **evitar** los trabajos pesados.
*The patient <u>should</u> **avoid** heavy work.*

60

Questions words

A statement "Carlos necesita un libro" *(Carlos needs a book)* can become a question by adding a question mark at the beginning and at the end of the sentence "¿Carlos necesita un libro?" *(Does Carlos need a book?)*. Look at the other possible ways:

Notice how the subject "Carlos" can change the position in a question.

1. ¿**Carlos** necesita un libro?
2. ¿Necesita **Carlos** un libro?   *Does Carlos need a book?*
3. ¿Necesita un libro **Carlos**?

Affirmative answer:

Si, Carlos necesita un libro
Yes, Carlos needs a book.

If the answer is negative, add the word NO before the verb in the sentence. When answering a question, an option is use a double negative. The first NO is for emphasis (It can be voided), the second NO makes the sentence negative and it is required.

No, no necesita un libro.
No, he does not need a book.

Questions can also be formed by adding the tags ¿no? or ¿verdad?

Ustedes trabajan los sábados, **¿verdad?**
You (all) work on Saturdays, right?

Tú hablas inglés, **¿no?**
You speak Engish, don't you?

In Spanish auxiliary verbs (do, does, will…) are not used when asking questions. Instead, an upside down question mark is used.

¿Dónde <u>le duele</u>?   *Where does it hurt?*

¿<u>Le duele</u> la cabeza?   *Does your head hurt?*

Question words are used to obtain different kinds of information. All question words bear a written accent over the stressed vowel.

¿Cómo?	How? (Sometimes what?)
¿Cuál(es)?	Which one(s)?
¿Cuándo?	When?
¿Cuánto/a?	How much?
¿Cuántos/as?	How many?
¿Dónde?	Where?
¿De dónde?	From where?
¿Adónde?	To where?
¿Por qué?	Why?
¿Qué?	What?
¿Quién(es)?	Who (all)?
¿De quién(es)?	Whose?
¿Para qué?	What for?

Some *question words* can have more than one meaning, for example "cómo."

¿Cómo está?	**How** are you?
¿Cómo se llama?	**What** is your name?

"Porque" is translated as "because" and "¿Por qué...?" (two words) as "Why...?"

¿Por qué necesitas una cita?
Why do you need an appointment?

Porque estoy enfermo.
Because I'm sick.

Verb "estar" *(The other verb TO BE)*

The verb "estar" is an irregular verb. It is irregular in the first person (Yo) and then it is conjugated the same way as a regular AR verb.

Yo	**estoy**	*I'm*
Tú	**estás**	*You are*
El		*He is*
Ella	**está**	*She is*
Ud.		*You are*
Nosotros/as	**estamos**	*We are*
Vosotros/as	**estáis**	*You are*
Ellos		*They are*
Ellas	**están**	*They are*
Uds.		*You are*

The verb "estar" is used with **adjectives** to talk about how people feel; it describes emotions, feelings and physical conditions.

List of adjectives

aburrido/a	*bored*
cansado/a	*tired*
cómodo/a	*comfortable*
deprimido/a	*depressed*
delgado/a	*thin*
enfermo/a	*sick*
enojado/a	*angry*
embarazada	*pregnant*
contento/a	*happy*
límpio/a	*clean*
nervioso/a	*nervous*

63

ocupado/a	busy
preocupado/a	worried
sucio/a	dirty
pálido/a	pale
triste	sad
feliz	happy

Adjectives agree in gender and number with a noun. The adjective "enferma" ends in "a" for a female and ends in "o" for a male. When referring to more than one person, the adjective is used in the plural form. The adjective "enfermo" has four different forms as in the example below:

Ana está <u>enferma</u>.	*Ana is sick.*
Carlos está <u>enfermo</u>.	*Carlos is sick.*
Ana y Carlos están <u>enfermos</u>.	*Ana and Carlos are sick.*
Ana y María están <u>enfermas</u>.	*Ana and Mary are sick.*
Las pacientes están enfermas.	*The patients are sick.*

If the adjective ends in 'e' then there are only two forms, the singular and the plural.

El paciente está **triste**.	*The patient is sad.* (Male)
La paciente está **triste**.	*The patient is sad.* (Female)
Los pacientes están **tristes**.	*The patients are sad.*
Las pacientes están **tristes**.	*The patients are sad.*

Use the verb "estar" to answer the question ¿Cómo está usted? (*How are you?)* or ¿Cómo está el paciente? (*How is the patient?)*

¿Cómo está usted?
(Yo) estoy cansado - *I'm tired*

¿Cómo está el paciente?
El paciente está enfermo- *The patient is sick*

The verb "estar" is also used to say where people, places and things are located.

¿Dónde está el paciente?
Where is the patient?

El paciente está en la sala de emergencia.
The patient is in emergency room.

¿Dónde está el hospital?
Where is the hospital?

El hospital está en Danvers.
The hospital is in Danvers.

Diálogos

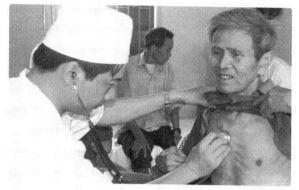

An appointment with the primary care physician

For translation of dialogs refer to Appendix 9.

Diálogo 1

Enfermera:	Sr. Ortiz, hablo español.
	No necesitamos un intérprete. ¿Cuánto pesa?
Paciente:	Yo peso 180 libras.
Enfermera:	¿Cuánto mide?
Paciente:	Mido 5 pies, siete pulgadas.
Enfermera:	¿Cómo se siente?
Paciente:	No muy bien.

Diálogo 2

Doctor:	¿Dónde le duele?
Paciente:	Me duele el estómago.
Doctor:	¿Le duele mucho o poco?
Paciente:	Me duele mucho.
Doctor:	De 1 a 10 ¿Cuánto le duele?
Paciente:	Ocho.
Doctor:	¿Puede describir el dolor?
Paciente:	El dolor es agudo.
Doctor:	¿Toma alguna medicina?
Paciente:	Tomo medicina para la diabetes.

Diálogo 3

Doctor: ¿Usted fuma?
Paciente: Si, fumo un poco.
Doctor: ¿Ud. tose mucho?
Paciente: Si, toso mucho.
Doctor: ¿Usted vomita?
Paciente: Si, vomito.
Doctor: ¿Usted vomita sangre?
Paciente: Si, vomito sangre a veces.
Doctor: ¿Dónde le duele?
Paciente: Me duele la espalda y la garganta.
Doctor: ¿El dolor es fuerte?
Paciente: El dolor es fuerte en mi espalda.
Doctor: Ud. Necesita unos análisis.

Diálogo 4   Un paciente con problemas de presión alta.

Doctora: ¿Cómo está Sr. Pérez?
Paciente: Estoy cansado, tengo dolor de cabeza y también tengo mareos.
Doctora: ¿Desde cuándo tiene dolor de cabeza?
Paciente: Una semana doctor.
Doctora: ¿Dónde le duele?
Paciente: Aquí, en mi frente.
Doctora: ¿Tiene los tobillos inflamados?
Paciente: Si, mis tobillos están inflamados por las noches.
Doctora: ¿Tiene sangrado de nariz?
Paciente: Sí, un poco.
Doctora: ¿Come mucha sal en las comidas? ¿Toma bebidas alcohólicas?
Paciente: Sí, me gusta la sal y bebo vino.
Doctora: En su hoja clínica su presión arterial es alta. Necesita una receta. Le aconsejo hablar con una dietista para cambiar su dieta.

Vocabulario

La dieta	*Diet*
Sal	*Salt*
Vino	*Wine*
Alguna	*Any*
Algo	*Something*
La hoja clínica/la historia clínica	*The medical history*
Un poco de español	*A little Spanish*
Bebidas alcohólicas	*Alcoholic beverages*
Me gusta la sal.	*I like salt.*
Necesita una receta médica.	*You need a prescription.*
Le aconsejo hablar con…	*I advise you to talk with…*
Tengo tobillos inflamados/hinchados.	*I have swollen ankles.*
La presión arterial alta/baja	*High/low blood pressure*
(Yo) mido 5 pies, una pulgada.	*I'm 5 feet, one inch.*
(Yo) peso 180 libras.	*I weigh 180 pounds.*

Preguntas

¿Tiene sangrado?	*Are you bleeding?*
¿Tiene mareos?	*Are you dizzy?*
¿Cuánto mide?	*How tall are you?*
¿Cuánto pesa?	*How much do you weigh?*
¿Puede describir el dolor?	*¿Could you describe the pain?*
¿Desde cuándo tiene …?	*Since when have you had …?*

¿Dónde le duele?	*Where does it hurt?*
Me duele aquí.	*It hurts here.*
Aqui, en la frente.	*Here in the forehead.*
Me duele el estómago.	*My stomach hurts.*
Me duelen las piernas.	*My legs hurt.*
¿Cuándo le duele?	*When does it hurt?*
Me duele cuando camino.	*It hurts when I walk.*
Me duele constantemente.	*It hurts constantly.*
¿Cuánto le duele?	*How much does it hurt?*
Me duele mucho.	*It hurts very much.*
Me duele un poco.	*It hurts a little.*
¿Puede describir el dolor? **¿Cómo es el dolor?**	*Can you describe the pain?*
El dolor es...	*The pain is...*
fuerte	*strong*
suave	*soft*
constante	*constant*
agudo	*sharp*
¿Dónde le duele al paciente?	*Where does it hurt on the patient?*
Le duele el brazo.	*His/her arm hurts.*
Le duele la garganta.	*His/her throat hurts.*

...de 1 a 10 ¿Cuánto le duele?
...from 1 to 10 how much does it hurt?

¿Cómo está el paciente?	How is the patient?

El paciente está...   The patient is...

delgado/a	thin
enfermo/a	sick
embarazada	pregnant
limpio/a	clean
nervioso/a	nervous
preocupado/a	worried
sucio/a	dirty
pálido/a	pale
triste	sad

¿Dónde está el paciente?	Where is the patient?

El paciente está en...   The patient is at...

el hospital	the hospital
la sala de emergencia	emergency room
la clínica	clinic
su casa	his/her house

¿Dónde está el hospital?	Where is the hospital?

El hospital está en Danvers.   The hospital is in Danvers.

Práctica

1. Find 10 cognates in the dialogs and list them below.

    a. _____

    b. _____

    c. _____

    d. _____

e. _____

f. _____

g. _____

h. _____

i. _____

j. _____

2. Match the following verbs with their corresponding equivalent.

   Verbs that end in AR

   a. Caminar   _____to work

   b. Regresar   _____to look for

   c. Desear   _____to speak

   d. Firmar   _____to sign

   e. Vacunar   _____to arrive

   f. Hablar   _____to wish/to want

   g. Llegar   _____to vaccinate

   h. Buscar   _____to return

   i. Trabajar   _____to walk

   Verbs that end in **IR**

   a. Escribir   _____to suffer

   b. Abrir   _____to write

   c. Vivir   _____to open

   d. Sufrir   _____to live

71

Verbs that end in **ER**

a. Apren**der** _____to eat

b. Be**ber** _____to read

c. Co**mer** _____to learn

d. De**ber** _____ to sell

e. Le**er** _____to drink

f. To**ser** _____owe/should/must

g. Ven**der** _____to cough

3. Complete each sentence with the correct form of the verbs in parentheses.

a. Juan y Maria _____de llenar la forma. (terminar)

b. La recepcionista_____en la planilla. (escribir)

c. La paciente_____ un mamograma. (necesitar)

d. El paciente_____mucho. (toser)

e. Jorge y yo _____en el Hospital General. (trabajar)

f. Usted _____matematicas y biologia? (estudiar)

g. Yo _____café. (desear)

h. Ella _____leche. (milk) (desear)

i. Nosotros_____ Español con los pacientes. (hablar)

j. La doctora Palacios_____ en la Clínica MAYO. (trabajar)

k. La paciente _____regresar mañana. (deber)

l. La paciente _____de insomnia. (sufrir)

m. ¿Tú_____ leche o limonada? (tomar)

n. Nosotros _____a la clase. (entrar)

o. Ellos_____ las planillas. (llenar)

p. Yo _____ los chocolates. (comprar)

q. El Sr. Vera no _____en Nueva York. (vivir)

r. Tú _____español con el médico. (hablar)

s. Nosotros_____ el español. (aprender)

t. El médico _____las radiografías. (necesitar)

u. Los pacientes_____ a las doce en punto. (comer)

v. ¿Qué idioma _____ustedes? (estudiar)

w. Nosotros_____ español. (estudiar)

x. ¿Qué_____ tú? (necesitar)

y. El doctor no_____ café. (beber)

z. El paciente_____leche descremada. (beber)

aa. Yo_____un libro. (comprar)

bb. ¿Ellos _____la cuenta? (pagar)

cc. El paciente _____un examen de orina.(necesitar)

dd. Los pacientes _____unos análisis de sangre.(necesitar)

4. Match the questions with the corresponding answers.

    a. ¿Cuánto mide?   _____ Yo peso 120 libras.

    b. ¿Dónde le duele?   _____ Mido 5 pies, dos pulgadas.

    c. ¿Cuánto le duele?   _____Estoy deprimido.

    d. ¿Toma alguna medicina? _____Me duele el cuello.

    e. ¿Cuánto pesa?   _____Me duele poco.

    f. ¿Cómo es el dolor?   _____El dolor es fuerte.

    g. ¿Cómo se siente?   _____Tomo aspirina.

5. Match the Spanish phrases with its English equivalent.

    a. El dolor es agudo.   _____The pain is constant.

    b. El dolor es suave.   _____The pain is sharp.

    c. El dolor es constante. _____The pain is strong.

    d. El dolor es fuerte.   _____The pain is soft.

6. Form questions with the following *question words*.

    a. ¿Cuánto   _____ siente?

    b. ¿Dónde le   _____ mide?

    c. ¿Cómo   _____ tiene dolor de cabeza?

    d. ¿Cómo se   _____ es el dolor?

    e. ¿Desde cuándo   _____ duele?

7. Complete the following sentences using the verb "estar" and the adjective in parenthesis. The adjectives should agree in gender and number with the noun.

Modelo: La paciente_____. *(delgado)*
          La paciente está delgada.

a.   El paciente no_____. *(preocupado)*

b.   La Sra. Vera _____. *(cansado)*

c.   Los niños (children) _____. *(aburrido)*

d.   La paciente _____. *(cómodo)*

e.   Yo no _____. *(enojado)*

f.   Nosotros _____. *(límpio)*

8. Answer the following questions.

a.   ¿Cómo se siente?_____.

b.   ¿Cuánto pesa?_____.

c.   ¿Cuánto mide?_____.

d.   ¿Dónde le duele?_____.

e.   ¿Cómo es el dolor?_____.

f.   ¿Usted fuma?_____.

g.   ¿Ud. tose?_____.

h.   ¿Está cansada?_____.

i.   ¿Tiene los tobillos inflamados?_____.

j.   ¿Tiene sangrado de nariz?_____.

k.   ¿Come mucha sal?_____.

l.   ¿Toma bebidas alcohólicas?_____.

9. What would you say in the following situations?

   a.   You are the nurse. Ask the patient how much she weighs, how tall she is and how she feels.

   b.   Ask the patient if she smokes and whether she takes any medicine.

   c.   Ask the patient if she eats a lot of salt.

   d.   Ask the patient if he drinks alcoholic beverages.

   e.   You are the doctor. Ask the patient where it hurts and how painful it is.

   f.   You are the patient. Tell the doctor that your knee hurts when you walk.

   g.   Tell the doctor that the pain is sharp and strong.

   h.   Tell the doctor that the patient takes medicine for diabetes and he is very tired and dizzy.

i. Tell the doctor that the patient's ankles are swollen and the pain is very strong.

j. Tell the nurse that the patient is pale, thin and that he is in the emergency room.

10. **Reporte**: You are a nurse, read the following dialog and write a report in Spanish about the patient. Describe his symptoms.

Diálogo 4   El paciente con problemas de presión

Doctora:	¿Cómo está Sr. Pérez?
Paciente:	Estoy cansado, tengo dolor de cabeza y también mareos.
Doctora:	¿Desde cuándo tiene dolor de cabeza?
Paciente:	Una semana doctor.
Doctora:	¿Dónde le duele?
Paciente:	Aquí, en la frente.
Doctora:	¿Tiene los tobillos inflamados?
Paciente:	Si, mis tobillos están inflamados por las noches.
Doctora:	¿Tiene sangrado de nariz?
Paciente:	Sí, un poco.
Doctora:	¿Come mucha sal en las comidas y toma bebidas alcohólicas?
Paciente:	Sí, me gusta la sal y bebo vino.
Doctora:	En la hoja clínica su presión arterial es alta. Necesita una receta médica. Le aconsejo hablar con la dietista para cambiar su dieta.

Start your report saying: El paciente...

Cultural Notes

Hispanic patients and health care professionals

In the United States not all Hispanics can afford health care. Even if they qualify for health insurance they prefer to find their own way of natural treatment first. It is customary to rely on elder family members who know how to treat different sicknesses through traditional healing methods. The last option is to purchase drugs prescribed by doctors.

Hispanics usually do not trust a health care professional who does not show interest in knowing a patient as a person. In Hispanic culture, trust is important before disclosing private information. It is crucial to take time to get to know the patient, to make them feel understood, and to help them comprehend the medical information given to them. If the health care professional does not speak Spanish, the service of an interpreter is imperative. If at all possible the interpreter should not be a family member.

LESSON 4 Conversando con la nutricionista.
Una dieta saludable.
Talking with the dietitian. A healthy diet.

Gramática

- Verb "gustar"
- Verb "poder"
- Impersonal Expressions

The verb "gustar"

Gustar means "to like." This is a two-word verb similar to "doler." The verb *gustar* does not use the pronouns "yo, tú, él, etc." instead, it uses the indirect object pronouns (me, te, le, nos, os, les). It also has two endings: the singular form that ends in "a" and the plural form that ends in "an."

Examples:

Me gusta el español.	*I like Spanish.*
Me gustan las enfermeras.	*I like the nurses.*

"Me gusta el español" is literally translated as "Spanish is pleasing to me." The proper English equivalent is "I like Spanish."

Conjugation of the verb Gustar

Singular	Plural	
Me gusta	Me gustan	*I like*
Te gusta	Te gustan	*You like*
Le gusta	Le gustan	*She likes, he likes, you like (formal)*
Nos gusta	Nos gustan	*We like*
Os gusta	Os gustan	*You like (plural informal Spain)*
Les gusta	Les gustan	*They like, you like (plural)*

Example:

¿Te gusta el café?   Sí, me gusta el café.
Do you like coffee?   *Yes, I like coffee.*

¿Le gustan los huevos?   Si, me gustan los huevos.
Do you like eggs?   *Yes, I like eggs.*

Use the singular form (me gusta) when the verb 'gustar' is followed by a second verb. The second verb is used in the infinitive form (without any endings).

Examples:

Me gusta <u>comer</u> arroz con pollo.
I like to eat rice with chicken.

¿Qué te gusta <u>beber</u>?   Me gusta beber té.
What do you like to drink? *I like to drink tea.*

The verb "poder"

The verb "poder" means "to be able to" and it is translated as "can" or "could." It is usually followed by another verb in the infinitive form. The verb "poder" is conjugated as an ER verb, but there are also changes in the root. The "o" changes into "ue" except in nosotros and vosotros.

Yo	puedo	I can
Tú	puedes	You can
El		He can
Ella	puede	She can
Ud.		You can
Nosotros	podemos	We can
Vosotros	podéis	You can
Ellos		They can
Ellas	pueden	They can
Uds.		You can

¿Qué puedo comer?
What can/could I eat?

Puede comer vegetales y fruta.
You can eat vegetables and fruit.

¿(yo) Puedo comer aguacates?
Can/Could I eat avocados?

Sí, (usted) puede comer aguacates.
Yes, you can eat avocados.

¿Puedo beber bebidas alcohólicas?
Can/Could I drink alcoholic beverages?

> No, no puede beber bebidas alcohólicas.
> *No, you can not drink alcoholic beverages.*

Impersonal expressions

The impersonal expression "**Es importante...**" is followed by a second verb in the infinitive form to state an opinion, to make indirect or subtle suggestions, or to suggest that something should be done without indicating who should do it.

Example:

1. Es importante contar las calorías.

   It is important to count the calories.

2. Es importante comer cantidades pequeñas.

   It is important to eat small portions.

You can also combine the sentences:

> **Es importante** contar las calorías y comer cantidades pequeñas.
> *It is important to count the calories and eat small portions.*

Example:

1. Es importante hacer ejercicio.
   It is important to exercise.

2. Es importante bajar de peso.
   It is important to lose weight.

> **Es importante** hacer ejercicio y bajar de peso.
> It is important to exercise and lose weight.

Diálogos

Talking with the dietitian. A healthy diet.

For translation of dialogs refer to Appendix 9.

En el hospital

Diálogo 1   La dietista

Dietista: Buenos días Srta. Vera. ¿Cómo está?

Paciente: Bien. Gracias.

Dietista: Para el desayuno tenemos cereal con leche y yogur.

Paciente: ¿Puedo desayunar huevos y pan tostado?

Dietista: Es importante evitar comidas con grasa y tener una dieta balanceada. ¿Qué bebe generalmente?

Paciente: Me gusta beber café. Bebo café descafeinado.

Dietista: Le aconsejo beber leche descremada o batido de frutas.

Diálogo 2

Dietista: ¿Qué desea almorzar?

Paciente: No tengo hambre.

Dietista: Es importante comer algo. Le aconsejo comer arroz al vapor con pollo y beber agua.

Paciente: No me gusta el agua.

Diálogo 3

Dietista: Sr. Pérez su hijo debe evitar el azúcar y comidas con grasa porque tiene sobrepeso y está desnutrido.

Sr. Pérez: ¿Qué debo hacer?

Dietista: Es importante comer en cantidades pequeñas, evitar comidas con grasa y sodas.

Sr. Pérez: ¿Qué puede comer?

Dietista: Su hijo puede comer vegetales y frutas. Aquí está la lista de alimentos.

Diálogo 4

Paciente: Necesito perder peso.

Dietista: ¿Qué come generalmente?

Paciente: Generalmente como dulces, tortas y bebo soda.

Dietista: Para evitar problemas del corazón y diabetes debe tener una dieta estricta.

Paciente: ¡Es muy difícil!

Dietista: Sí, pero es importante bajar de peso. Aquí hay una lista de alimentos para usted. Es importante contar las calorías y hacer ejercicio.

Vocabulario

No tengo apetito.	*I do not have an appetite.*
No tengo hambre.	*I'm not hungry*
Necesito perder peso.	*I need to lose weight.*
Aquí está la lista de alimentos.	*Here is a list of healthy food.*
No me gusta el jugo de manzana.	*I do not like apple juice.*
Ud. está desnutrido.	*You're malnourished.*
El/ella está desnutrido/a	*He/she is malnourished.*
Ud. tiene sobrepeso.	*You are overweight.*
El/ella tiene sobrepeso	*He/she is overweight.*
Ud. debe evitar…	*You should avoid…,*
El/ella debe evitar…	*He/she should avoid…*

Para evitar problemas de corazón…
In order to avoid heart problems…

Para evitar problemas de diabetes…
In order to avoid diabetes …

Verbos

Almorzar (stem-changing verb)	*To have lunch*
Cenar	*To have dinner*
Desayunar	*To have breakfast*
Seguir (irregular/stem-changing verb)	*To follow*

To state your opinion use this phrase: "Es importante…"

Es importante comer…   *It is important to eat …*

    cantidades pequeñas   *small portions*

    vegetales y frutas   *vegetables and fruits*

    menos   *less*

    algo   *something*

Es importante …   *It is important…*

    bajar de peso   *to lose weight*

    contar las calorías   *count caloric intake*

    hacer ejercicio   *to exercise*

    asar la carne   *to grill the meat*

    cocinar al vapor   *to steam*

    cocinar al horno   *to bake*

    tomar mucho líquido   *to drink lots of liquids*

Es importante evitar…   *It is important to avoid…*

    Comidas con grasa/   *greasy food*
    comidas grasosas

    comidas fritas   *fried foods*

    el azúcar   *sugar*

    comidas picantes   *spicy foods*
    comidas condimentadas

    las sodas   *sodas*

Es importante tener una dieta... *It's important to have a_____ diet*

balanceada	*balanced*
estricta	*strict*
con poca grasa	*low fat*
sin sal	*without salt*
especial	*special*

To give advice: "Le aconsejo.../No le aconsejo...

Le aconsejo beber...   *I advise you to drink...*

mucho líquido	*lots of liquids*
agua	*water*
leche descremada	*low fat milk*
jugos sin azucar	*juices without sugar*
jugo de fresas	*strawberry juice*
batidos de fruta	*fruit smoothies*

No le aconsejo beber   *I would not advise you to drink...*

cerveza	*beer*
vino	*wine*
bebidas alcohólicas	*alcoholic beverages*

Le aconsejo comer...   *I advise you to eat...*

frutas	*fruits*
bananas	*bananas*
fresas	*strawberries*

manzanas	*apples*
naranjas	*oranges*
vegetales	*vegetables*
bróculi, brécol	*broccoli*
cereal	*cereal*
ensalada con tomate	*salad with tomato*
aguacate/palta	*avocado*

No le aconsejo comer... — *I would not advise you to eat...*

mucha sal	*too much salt*
dulces	*sweets*

Preguntas

¿Qué come generalmente? — *What do you generally eat?*
(Yo) como... — *I eat...*

tortillas con queso	*tortillas with cheese*
mantequilla de maní	*peanut butter*

¿Qué desea desayunar?
What do you like to have for breakfast?

(Yo) deseo comer — *I would like to eat... (I want to have...)*
El paciente desea... — *The patient would like...*

huevos	*eggs*
pan	*bread*
pan tostado	*toast*
tostada con mantequilla	*toast with butter*
yogur	*yogurt*

Yo desayuno cereal con leche.   *I have cereal and milk for breakfast.*

¿Qué desea almorzar?   *What would you like for lunch?*
What do you want to have for lunch?

(Yo) deseo…   *I want…*
El paciente desea…   *The patient wants…*

una hamburguesa	*a hamburger*
arroz con pollo	*rice with chicken*
pasta/fideos	*pasta*
espaguetis	*spaghetti*
frijoles	*beans*
pescado	*fish*

¿Qué desea cenar?
What would you like for dinner?

Yo deseo cenar arroz con pollo.
I'll have rice with chicken for dinner.

El paciente desea cenar arroz con pollo
The patient wants to eat rice with chicken for dinner.

¿Qué debo comer?   *What should I eat?*

Usted debe comer vegetales y frutas.
You should eat vegetables and fruits.

El paciente debe comer vegetales y frutas.
The patient should eat vegetables and fruits.

Práctica

1. Find 10 cognates in the dialogs and list them below.

   a. _____

   b. _____

   c. _____

   d. _____

   e. _____

   f. _____

   g. _____

   h. _____

   i. _____

   j. _____

2. Complete the following dialog with the verbs provided.

   Desear/cenar

   ¿Qué _____ cenar hoy?

   Yo _____arroz con pollo y jugo de naranja.

Deber

¿Qué _____ hacer doctor?

Ud. _____ seguir una dieta balanceada.

Cocinar

¿Uds. _____ al vapor o al horno?

Nosotros _____al vapor.

Tomar

¿El paciente _____ mucho o poco líquido?

Comer

¿Qué _____el Sr. y la Sra. Vera?

Ellos_____ cereal con leche descremada.

Ser/Estar

El paciente _____desnutrido.

_____importante comer vegetales y frutas.

3. Complete the following sentences with the verb provided.

   a. La paciente _____estar a dieta. *(necesitar)*

   b. Yo_____ triste *(estar)*

c. El doctor no_____ un intérprete. *(necesitar)*

d. Nosotros no _____medicinas *(tomar)*

e. El paciente_____ mucho. *(toser)*

f. Mis tobillos no _____ inflamados. *(estar)*

g. ¿Usted_____ los tobillos hinchados? *(tener)*

h. ¿El paciente _____mucha sal? *(comer)*

i. ¿Usted_____ bebidas alcohólicas? *(tomar)*

j. Su presión arterial_____ alta. *(ser)*

k. El paciente _____una receta. *(necesitar)*

l. Nosotros _____cansados. *(estar)*

m. Las enfermeras_____ preocupadas. *(estar)*

n. Yo_____ cansado. *(estar)*

o. Ellos _____en Danvers, MA. *(vivir)*

p. (yo) _____la espalda. *(doler)*

q. La paciente_____ sangrado de naríz. *(tener)*

r. ¿Usted_____dolor de cabeza? *(tener)*

s. El paciente_____ 180 libras. *(pesar)*

t. El paciente _____5pies, ocho pulgadas. *(medir)*

u. Los doctores no _____español. *(hablar)*

v. ¿El paciente _____ sangrado? *(tener)*

w. ¿Cómo_____ el paciente? *(estar)*

x. El paciente_____ pálido. *(estar)*

y. ¿Dónde_____el hospital? *(estar)*

z. El hospital_____ en Danvers, MA. *(estar)*

4. Match the Spanish phrases with the English phrases.

a. Está desnutrido.   _____I do not have an appetite

b. No tengo apetito.   _____You should avoid

c. Tiene sobrepeso...   _____He/she is overweight

d. Debe evitar...   _____He/she is malnourished.

e. Para evitar...   _____I need to lose weight

f. Necesito perder peso.   _____In order to avoid

5. Answer the following questions in complete sentences.

a. ¿Cómo está?

b. ¿Qué desea desayunar?

c. ¿Qué desea almorzar?

d. ¿Qué desea cenar?

e. ¿Qué desea beber?

f. ¿Qué come generalmente?

6. Write a complete menu for a patient who needs to lose weight. Add healthy foods and drinks.

   a. El desayuno

   b. El almuerzo

   c. La cena

7. What would you say in the following situations?

   a. Advise the patient to avoid alcoholic beverages.

   b. Tell the patient that you are the dietitian. Tell him that he needs to lose weight and that it is important to be on a diet.

   c. Tell the doctor that the patient is overweight and malnourished.

   d. Tell the doctor that the patient is not hungry.

   e. You are the dietitian. Tell the patient that it is important to eat small portions.

   f. Tell the patient that it is important to exercise and lose weight.

   g. Tell the patient that he must avoid greasy and spicy foods.

   h. Advise the patient to eat fruits and vegetables.

i. Tell the patient that it is important to steam the food.

j. Advise the patient to drink lots of liquids.

k. Advise the patient what to eat for dinner.

l. Tell the patient that in order to avoid heart problems; he needs to follow a strict diet.

8. You are the nurse. Tell the mother of a child that he is malnourished and overweight. He needs to eat vegetables and fruit. Tell her that it is important to avoid greasy foods, fried foods, and sugar. Finally, tell her that it is important to follow a diet.

   Respuesta: Señora Vera, su hijo…

Obesity and Hispanics in the USA

Obesity is considered an epidemic in the United States. A large percentage of the Hispanic community is overweight or obese. These communities are a popular target for fast-food companies. Via TV commercials and advertisements, companies are enticing viewers to believe their foods are the healthy and most economical choice. Many Hispanics are not aware of the detrimental consequences of eating unhealthy. This is usually because in their countries, *las meriendas* (snacks) and their fast-food restaurants serve healthier foods than what people consume in the USA.

It is crucial to educate Hispanics about how low nutritional foods and lack of exercise impact their health. If they are given sufficient information and have a Spanish speaker explain the diseases and dreadful outcomes then there is an increased chance that they will cooperate.

Brenda A. Palacios

Kit para el cuidado cardiovascular

Cada año una de cada cuatro muertes es causada por problemas cardiovasculares.

Hacer ejercicios.

Seguir una dieta saludable.

Dormir lo suficiente.

Brenda A. Palacios

Enfermedades cardiovasculares

La mayoría de las enfermedades cardiovasculares ECV pueden prevenirse aumentando la actividad física, evitando el consumo de tabaco y alcohol, reduciendo la sal en las comidas y llevando una dieta rica en frutas y vegetales. También puede ser necesario prescribir un tratamiento farmacológico para la diabetes, la hipertensión o la hiperlipidemia, con el fin de reducir el riesgo cardiovascular y prevenir ataques cardíacos y accidentes cerebrovasculares.

Síntomas Comunes de un Ataque Cardiaco

– Presión incómoda
– Sensación de estar lleno o dolor insoportable en el pecho que se extiende al cuello, la mandíbula, los hombros y los brazos
– Mareos o sensación de perder el sentido
– Incremento de sudor
– Falta de aire
– Nausea
– Desmayo

Síntomas Comunes de una Embolia

– Adormecimiento o debilitamiento en el rostro, el brazo o la pierna Confusión, problemas para hablar o entender
– Problemas para ver con uno o con los dos ojos
– Problemas para caminar, mareo, falta de balance o coordinación
– Dolor de cabeza severo sin causa alguna

Gramática

- Irregular verbs
- Expressions with verb "tener"
- Impersonal verb "hay"

Irregular Verbs

Irregular verbs do not follow a pattern. Their conjugations must be memorized. The following verbs are irregular only in the "yo" form. Refer to Appendix 12 for more irregular verbs.

Dar	*to give*
Conocer	*to be acquainted with/ to meet*
Hacer	*to do; to make*
Poner	*to put; to place*

	dar	conocer	hacer	poner
yo	doy	conozco	hago	pongo
tú	das	conoces	haces	pones
él ella Ud.	da	conoce	hace	pone
nosotros/as	damos	conocemos	hacemos	ponemos
vosotros/as	dais	conocéis	hacéis	ponéis
ellos ellas Uds.	dan	conocen	hacen	ponen

98

Traer   *to bring*
Salir   *to go out, to leave*
Venir   *to come*
Ver   *to see*

	Traer	Salir	Venir	Ver
yo	tra**igo**	sal**go**	ven**go**	**veo**
tú	traes	sales	vienes	ves
él / ella / Ud.	trae	sale	viene	ve
nosotros/as	traemos	salimos	venimos	vemos
vosotros/as	traéis	salís	venís	veis
ellos / ellas / Uds.	traen	salen	vienen	ven

The verb *tener (to have)* and the verb *venir (to come)* are similar in their conjugation.

Verb "tener"

The verb "necesitar" *(to need)* and "deber" *(should/must)* are used to say what we need or should do.

El paciente **necesita** descansar.	*The patient needs to rest.*
El paciente **debe** descansar.	*The patient should rest.*

The verb "tener" is also an irregular verb. It has been previously used to indicate possession.

Example:

"Tengo una forma"   *I have a form*

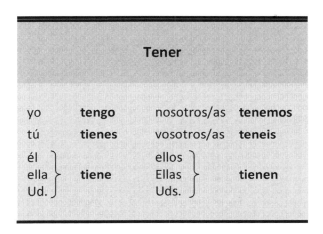

Tener			
yo	**tengo**	nosotros/as	**tenemos**
tú	**tienes**	vosotros/as	**teneis**
él ⎫		ellos ⎫	
ella ⎬	**tiene**	Ellas ⎬	**tienen**
Ud. ⎭		Uds. ⎭	

The verb *tener* can also be used to say what you have to do. Add the word 'que' when tener is followed by another verb. "que" does not have an equivalent in English.

Examples:

Yo tengo que descansar.   *I have to rest.*
El paciente tiene que descansar.   *The pacient has to rest.*

Expressions with the verb "tener"

Idiomatic expressions are sometimes hard to remember since the English translation requires the verb "to be" while Spanish uses the verb "tener."

tener hambre (f.)	to be hungry
tener mareos	to be dizzy
tener nausea	to be nauseated
tener sed (f.)	to be thirsty
tener sueño (m.)	to be sleepy
tener calor (m.)	to be hot
tener frío (m.)	to be cold
tener cuidado (m.)	to be careful
tener razón (f.)	to be right
tener prisa (f.)	to be in a hurry
tener miedo (m.)	to be afraid
tener vergüenza	to be embarrassed
tener éxito	to be successful
tener ___ años	to be ___ years old
tener ganas de...	to feel like ...

Examples:

El paciente tiene frío.   *The patient is cold.*
El paciente tiene hambre.   *The patient is hungry.*

To ask how old someone is, say:

¿Cuántos años tiene?   *How old are you?*
Tengo 20 años.   I'm twenty years old.

To say that you feel like doing something, use the expression "**tener ganas de...**"

El paciente tiene ganas de comer pollo.
The patient feels like eating chicken.

Nosotros <u>tenemos ganas de beber</u> agua.
We feel like drinking water.

La paciente <u>no tiene ganas de beber</u>.
The patient does not feel like drinking.

Impersonal verb "hay"

HAY has four different forms and meanings:

Is there...?	There is...
Are there...?	There are...

Examples:

Hay un doctor en la sala de emergencia.
***There is** one doctor at the emergency room.*

Hay cinco pacientes en la sala de emergencia.
***There are** five patients in the emergency room.*

¿**Hay** un doctor en el consultorio ahora?
***Is there** a doctor at the doctor's office right now?*

¿**Hay** muchas enfermeras en el hospital?
***Are there** many nurses at the hospital?*

To express the idea of "one must do something" or "it is necessary to do something" **Hay que + a verb in the infinitive** form must be used. It is used as a general statement without a specific subject.

Examples:

Hay que cuidar a los pacientes.
One must take care of the patients.

Hay que bajar de peso.
It is necessary to lose weight.

Diálogos

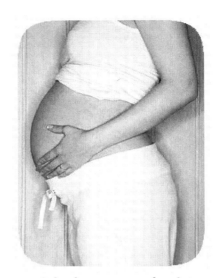

An appointment with the gynecologist

For translation of dialogs refer to Appendix 9.

Dialogo *1*   *La ginecóloga y la paciente embarazada*

Doctora: Sra. Vera, buenos días. ¿Cómo está?

Sra. Vera: No muy bien doctora.

Doctora: ¿Qué síntomas tiene?

Sra. Vera: No tengo la regla desde febrero.

Doctora: ¿Su regla es regular o irregular?

Sra. Vera: Es regular, doctora.

Doctora: Bien. ¿Tiene mareos? ¿Tiene nausea? ¿Está cansada?

Sra. Vera: Si, tengo mareos y nausea. Siempre estoy cansada.

Doctora: ¿Usted vomita?

Sra. Vera: Vomito en las mañanas.

Doctora: ¿Sus senos están inflamados y duros?

Sra. Vera: Mis senos están hinchados y también duros.

Doctora: ¿Orina con frecuencia?

Sra. Vera: Sí, orino con frecuencia.

Doctora: Necesita una prueba de orina, un análisis de sangre y un examen vaginal.

Diálogo 2

Doctora: ¿Cuántos años tiene Sra. Pérez?

Sra. Pérez: Tengo 45 años, doctora.

Doctora: ¡Felicitaciones! Usted está embarazada. Hay que tener cuidado porque es un embarazo de alto riesgo.

Sra. Pérez: ¿Qué debo hacer, doctora?

Doctora: Tiene que seguir mis instrucciones.

Diálogo 3

Doctora: Sra. Vera, ¡Felicitaciones! Ud. está embarazada.

Sra. Vera: Gracias, doctora.

Doctora: ¿Usted fuma?

Sra. Vera: Si, fumo una cajetilla al día.

Doctora: Tiene que dejar de fumar porque es malo para el bebé y para usted también.

Sra. Vera: Muy bien, doctora.

Doctora: ¿Usted bebe bebidas alcohólicas?

Sra. Vera: Bebo muy poco.

Doctora: Debe evitar las bebidas alcohólicas. Tiene que descansar y evitar los trabajos pesados. Necesita tomar mucho líquido, evitar la cafeína, las sodas y drogas en general.

Sra. Vera: ¿Necesito una dieta?

Doctora: Sí, si tiene hambre debe comer mucha fruta y vegetales.

Sra. Vera: Muy bien doctora.

Doctora: Sra. Vera, necesita regresar el próximo mes.

Diálogo 4

Doctora: Sra. Poma, la enfermera trae su historia médica en un momento.

Sra. Poma: Gracias, doctora.

Doctora: ¿Usted viene para los análisis de sangre mañana?

Sra. Poma: Si, yo vengo mañana.

Al día siguiente: (the next day)

Doctora: Los resultados son negativos, Sra. Poma. Usted no está embarazada.

Diálogo 5

Centro de Planificación familiar/el control de la natalidad. La doctora habla con un grupo de mujeres jóvenes.

Doctora: Para evitar el embarazo necesita tomar las pastillas anticonceptivas. Hay también otros métodos.

Una joven: ¿Qué otros métodos hay para evitar el embarazo?

Doctora: El aparato intrauterino, la inyección mensual, los condones y la abstinencia. Las pastillas son más efectivas. Los condones son necesarios para evitar enfermedades. El aborto es una opción en caso de embarazo no deseado.

Vocabulario

El condón	*Condom*
La abstinencia	*Abstinence*
La regla, el periodo	*Menstrual period*
Las pastillas anticonceptivas	*Contraceptive pills*
El aparato intrauterino	*Intrauterine device (IUD)*
La prueba de orina	*Urine test*
La inyección mensual	*Monthly shot*
Si tiene hambre...	*If you are hungry...*
La paciente está embarazada.	*The patient is pregnant.*
El resultado es negativo.	*The test is negative.*
El resultado es positivo.	*The test is positive.*
Para evitar el embarazo	*To avoid pregnancy*
La historia médica	*Medical file (medical history)*
Fumo una cajetilla al día.	*I smoke a pack a day.*
Evitar los trabajos pesados	*Avoid heavy work*
Bebidas alcohólicas	*Alcoholic beverages*
Mis senos están duros.	*My breasts are hard.*
Mis senos están inflamados/hinchados.	*My breasts are swollen.*
Necesita venir...	*You need to come...*

mañana.	*tomorrow.*
el lunes.	*on Monday.*
el próximo lunes.	*next Monday.*
la próxima semana.	*next week.*
el próximo mes.	*next month.*

Verbos

Vomitar	*To vomit*
Orinar	*To urinate*
Fumar	*To smoke*
Evitar	*To avoid*
Descansar	*To rest*

Preguntas

¿Tiene mareos?	*Are you dizzy?*
¿Tiene nausea?	*Are you nauseous?*
¿Está cansada?	*Are you tired?*

¿Qué síntomas tiene la paciente?
What are the patient's symptoms?

La paciente tiene...   *The patient has...*

nausea.	*nausea.*
mareos.	*dizziness.*
los tobillos inflamados.	*swollen ankles.*
los senos inflamados.	*swollen breasts.*

La paciente está...   *The patient is ...*

cansada.	*tired.*
triste.	*sad.*
contenta.	*happy.*
embarazada.	*pregnant.*

La paciente necesita...   *The patient needs...*

una prueba de orina.   *a urine test.*

un análisis de sangre.   *a blood test.*

un examen vaginal.   *a vaginal exam.*

La paciente tiene que...   *The patient has to...*

dejar de fumar.   *stop smoking.*

descansar.   *rest.*

tomar mucho líquido.   *drink a lot of liquids.*

dejar de beber bebidas alcohólicas.
stop drinking alcoholic beverages.

La paciente tiene que evitar...   *The patient has to avoid...*

los trabajos pesados.   *heavy work.*

las drogas.   *drugs.*

la cafeína.   *caffeine.*

el alcohol.   *alcohol.*

Práctica

1. Find 10 cognates in the dialogs and list them below.

a. _____

b. _____

c. _____

d. _____

e. _____

f. _____

g. _____

h. _____

i. _____

j. _____

2. Match the Spanish verbs with the English verbs.

a.	Dar	_____ to do, to make
b.	Conocer	_____ to have
c.	Venir	_____ to see, to watch
d.	Poner	_____ to put, to place
e.	Salir	_____ to bring
f.	Ver	_____ to come
g.	Tener	_____ to know/to meet
h.	Hacer	_____ to give
i.	Traer	_____ to leave, to go out

3. Complete the sentences with the correct conjugation of the following irregular verbs.

dar   conocer   venir   poner   traer   salir   ver

a. La enfermera _____ las pruebas de sangre al doctor.

b. Los pacientes _____ a la cita a las tres de la tarde.

c. El doctor _____ la inyección al paciente.

d. El Sr. Perez _____del hospital el cuatro de febrero.

e. ¿Usted _____ al doctor?

4. Choose the most appropriate expression for the following exercises.

tener hambre (f.)	*tener cuidado (m.)*
tener sed (f.)	*tener razón (f.)*
tener sueño (m.)	*tener prisa (f.)*
tener calor (m.)	*tener miedo (m.)*
tener frío (m.)	*tener vergüenza*
tener éxito	

a. The patient did not eat anything in 24 hours.

b. The patient has to have surgery.

c. The patient did not sleep well.

d. The patient is dehydrated.

e. The patient was scheduled to have surgery at 2:00. It is now 2:05. The nurse is late.

5. Answer the following questions.

   a. ¿Cuántos años tiene la paciente?

   b. ¿Cómo está la paciente?

   c. ¿La paciente tiene mareos?

   d. ¿Ella tiene los tobillos hinchados?

   e. ¿Qué examenes necesita?

   f. ¿Su regla es regular o irregular?

   g. ¿Tiene nausea?

   h. ¿Tiene los senos inflamados o duros?

   i. ¿Está cansada?

   j. ¿Orina con frecuencia?

   k. ¿Vomita?

6. What would you say in the following situations?

   a. Tell the patient that she needs a blood test, a urine test, and a vaginal exam.

   b. Tell the doctor that the patient has not had her period since February, she is nauseated and dizzy, she is always tired, and her breasts are swollen.

c. Congratulate the patient for her pregnancy and tell her that she has to follow your instructions.

d. Tell the patient to stop smoking. It is bad for the baby and for her.

e. Tell the patient to rest and avoid heavy work.

f. Tell the patient to drink plenty of liquids but to avoid caffeine, sodas, and any drugs.

g. Tell the patient that she should eat lots of fruits and vegetables.

h. Ask the patient if she is coming for a blood test tomorrow.

i. Tell a group of young women the different ways to avoid pregnancy.

j. Tell the patient that the tests are negative and she is not pregnant.

k. Ask the receptionist if there is a doctor in the office.

l. You are the patient. Tell the nurse what you feel like eating.

Cultural Notes

Family planning among Hispanics

Family planning is a sensitive topic among Hispanics and should be done in private. Many women use contraception without informing their husbands or family. This is a controversial and problematic topic since the majority of Hispanics are religious. Usually female relatives accompany women to prenatal care and play an important part through pregnancy and post natal care.

La cuarentena ("quarantine") is a forty day postpartum period. During this period of time female relatives take over errands and chores while the new mother recuperates from labor and bonds with the baby. No sex, heavy work or greasy foods are allowed during this time. The mother should not leave the house during the day to avoid heat and at night to avoid cold. Hispanics believe that proper observance leads to good health and old age.

LESSON 6 Una cita con el pediatra. Enfermedades, remedios y vacunas.

An appointment with the pediatrician. Sicknesses, remedies and vaccines.

Gramática

Saber vs. conocer
- Verb "ir"
- Ir + a + infinitive
- Ser vs. estar
- Affirmative and Negative Expressions

Saber vs. conocer

The verb *saber* and *conocer* are irregular verbs in the "yo" form. They can both be translated as "to know." However, they are not interchangeable.

	Saber	Conocer
yo	sé	conozco
tú	sabes	conoces
él ella Ud.	sabe	conoce
nosotros/as	sabemos	conocemos
vosotros/as	sabeis	conocéis
ellos ellas Uds.	saben	conocen

114

The verb "saber"

The verb "saber" is used to express skills or information already learned or not known information.

Examples:

El paciente sabe mi número de teléfono.
The patient knows my phone number.

El paciente no sabe mi número de teléfono.
The patient does not know my phone number.

El doctor sabe los resultados de los exámenes.
The doctor knows the tests results.

La enfermera sabe el número de teléfono del hospital.
The nurse knows the hospital's phone number.

The verb "saber" is used to say that you know how to do an activity such as driving, cooking, riding a bike or dancing.

Yo sé cocinar.   *I know how to cook.*
Sabemos tocar el piano.   *We know how to play the piano.*

"Saber" can be followed by a verb in the infinitive form.

El paciente <u>sabe conducir</u>.
The patient knows how to drive.

"Saber" can be followed by a question word.

Yo sé quién es el doctor.
I know who the doctor is.

The verb "conocer"

"Conocer" is used to say that one is or is not acquainted with a person, place or thing.

> El niño conoce la geografía Americana.
> *The boy is familiar with American geography.*

> *Conozco los poemas de Neruda.*
> *I'm familiar with Neruda's poems.*

> Conozco Boston.
> *I know Boston.*

To say that you know someone, the verb "conocer" is follow by the preposition "a."

> Conozco **a** la doctora.   *I know the doctor.*

Verb "ir" (to go)

The verb "ir" is an irregular verb and it is usually followed by the preposition "a."

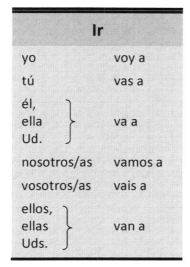

Ir	
yo	voy a
tú	vas a
él, ella Ud.	va a
nosotros/as	vamos a
vosotros/as	vais a
ellos, ellas Uds.	van a

It is used as an expression "vamos" or "vámonos" (let's go).
When the verb "ir" is followed by a second verb it is used to express an action that will take place in the future.

> Vamos a vacunar al niño la próxima semana.
> *We are going to vaccinate the child next week.*
> *We will vaccinate the child next week.*

vamos a – *(first verb) we are going to… (we'll go)*
vacunar – *(second verb) to vaccinate (not conjugated)*

Example:

> El paciente <u>va a mejorarse</u> pronto.
> *The patient <u>is going to get better</u> soon.*
> *The patient <u>will get better</u> soon.*

Verb "ser" and "estar"

To be	ser	estar
yo	soy	estoy
tú	eres	estás
él, ella Ud.	es	está
nosotros	somos	estamos
vosotros	sois	estáis
ellos ellas Uds.	son	están

Both verbs are irregular. The verb "ser" is used to say who you are, where you are from, and what your nationality is. It is also use to describe people, places or things *(Lesson 1)*.

The verb "estar" is used to say how people feel and how people, places and things are located *(Lesson 3)*.

"Ser" and "estar" used with adjectives

The verb "ser" describes permanent conditions.

El paciente es...   *The patient is*

    asmático/a   *asthmatic*
    delgado/a   *thin*
    alérgico/a (a la sulfa)   *allergic to sulfa*
    alérgico/a (a la penicilina)   *allergic to penicillin*
    gordo/a   *overweight/fat*

The verb "estar" describes temporary conditions.

El paciente está...   *The patient is...*

    delgado/a   *(looks) thin*
    pálido/a   *pale*
    enfermo/a   *sick*
    resfriado/a   *has a cold*
    gordo /a   *fat*
    estreñido/a   *constipated*
    aventado/hinchado/a   *bloated*
    anémico/a   *anemic*

Here is a list of adjectives that change meaning when used with the Spanish verbs "ser" or "estar."

    Estar aburrido   *to be bored*
    Ser aburrido   *to be boring*

Estar ciego	*to be temporarily blinded by something*
Ser ciego	*to be a blind person*
Estar débil	*to be weak*
Ser débil	*to be a weakling*
Estar delgado	*to look thin*
Ser delgado	*to be thin*
Estar frío	*to be cold in terms of temperature*
Ser frío	*to be unfeeling, frigid, cold (personality)*
Estar grave	*to be in poor health*
Ser grave	*to be serious*
Estar viejo	*to look old*
Ser viejo	*to be old*
Estar vivo	*to be alive*
Ser vivo	*to be clever*

The adjectives agree in gender and number with the noun.

El paciente está delgado	*The patient is (looks) thin.*
Los pacientes están delgados	*The patients are (look) thin.*
El paciente está pálido.	*The patient is (looks) pale.*
La paciente está pálida.	*The female patient is (looks) pale.*

Affirmative and Negative Expressions

Affirmative Expressions		Negative Expressions	
siempre	*always*	nunca	*never*
a veces	*sometimes*	jamás	*never*
algo	*something*	nada	*nothing*
alguien	*someone*	nadie	*nobody, no one*
algún	*anything*	ningún	*none*
alguno/a,	*some, any*	ninguno/a,	*none*
algunos/as	*some, any*	ningunos/as	*none*

Siempre, nunca, a veces, alguien and nadie are usually placed at the beginning of the sentence:

Examples:

(Yo) **siempre** estoy contento.
I am always happy.

(Yo) **nunca** como pollo.
I never eat chicken.

(Yo) **a veces** como vegetales.
I sometimes eat vegetables.

¿Hay **alguien** en la sala de emergencia?
Is there someone in the emergency room?

No hay **nadie** en la sala de emergencia.
There is no one in the emergency room.

The use of a double negative is quite common in Spanish.

Example:

No tengo **nada** que hacer.
I don't have anything to do.

No hay nada tampoco.
There is nothing either.

Diálogos

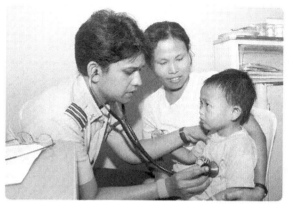

An appointment with the pediatrician. Sicknesses, remedies and vaccines

For translation of dialogs refer to Appendix 9.
El pediatra y los padres del niño

Diálogo 1

Pediatra: ¿Cómo está Juanito hoy?
Sra. Pérez: Juanito está enfermo, doctor.
Pediatra: ¿Cuáles son sus síntomas?
Sra. Pérez: Se frota mucho sus oídos.
Pediatra: ¿El niño tiene fiebre?
Sra. Pérez: Si, tiene 103 grados de temperatura y también catarro.
Pediatra: ¿Tiene tos?
Sra. Pérez: Si doctor. Tiene tos.
Pediatra: Voy a examinar a Juanito.

Después *(later)*
Pediatra: Juanito tiene una infección en los oídos. Hay pus y sangre en el oído izquierdo. Voy a recetar un antibiótico y un descongestionante. ¿El niño es alérgico a los antibióticos o descongestionantes?

Sra. Perez: No, doctor.

Diálogo 2

Sra. Pérez: Mi hijo está resfriado y tiene asma, doctor.

Pediatra: ¿Cuántos años tiene el niño?

Sra. Pérez: Tiene dos años.

Pediatra: El niño está muy delgado, Sra. Pérez. El sólo pesa 20 libras.

Sra. Pérez: Si, mi hijo come poco y siempre está estreñido y aventado.

Pediatra: Está muy pálido. El niño puede estar anémico. Necesita un análisis de sangre. Ud. necesita llevar al niño al laboratorio en ayunas. También debe hablar con la dietista.

Diálogo 3

Sra. Vera: ¿Qué necesita mi hija, doctor?

Pediatra: Ella necesita tomar tylenol para niños cada cuatro horas.

Diálogo 4

Enfermera: Sra. Vera su hijo necesita la vacuna contra el tétano, la tosferina y la difteria.

Sra. Vera: Muy bien.

Enfermera: También vamos a hacer una prueba contra la tuberculosis la próxima vez.

Vocabulario

Sólo pesa...	*Only weighs...*
La próxima vez...	*Next time...*
Oído izquierdo	*Left ear (internal)*
Oído derecho	*Right ear (internal)*

El niño puede estar anémico.
The child could be anemic.

Voy a examinar al niño.
I'm going to examine the child.

Voy a hacer una prueba de tuberculina.
I'm going to do a tuberculin test.

Voy a recetar un antibiótico.
I'm going to prescribe an antibiotic.

¿Cuáles son sus síntomas? *What are his/her/your symptoms?*

El paciente...   *The patient...*

frota sus oídos	*rubs his/her ears*
tiene fiebre	*he/she has a fever*
tiene catarro/está resfriado	*he/she has a cold*
tiene tos	*he/she has a cough*
tiene pus/hay pus	*he/she has pus*
tiene sangre en el oído	*he/she has blood in his/her ear*
tiene infección en los oídos	*he/she has an ear infection*
tiene asma	*has asthma*

Voy a vacunar al niño contra...
I'm going to vaccinate the child against...

El tétano	*tetanus*
La tos ferina	*whooping cough, pertussis*
La difteria	*diphtheria*

Voy a vacunar al niño contra el MMR
I'm to vaccinate one child against MMR

Las paperas	*mumps*
El sarampión	*measles*
La rubeola	*rubella*

¿Qué necesita mi hija? *What does my daughter need?*

La niña necesita.../la paciente necesita...
The child needs.../the patient needs...

una inyección	*a shot*
sulfa	*sulfa*

Tomar Pedialyte para la deshidratación.
to take Pedialyte for the dehydration.

un antibiótico para la infección.
an antibiotic for the infection.

Kaopectate para la diarrea.
Kaopectate for diarrhea.

ungüento/pomada para las nalgas irritadas.
ointment for irritated buttocks.

El paciente necesita tomar...	*The patient needs to take...*
un descongestionante	*a decongestant*
Tylenol para niños	*children's Tylenol*
la medicina	*medicine*
la aspirina	*aspirin*
la tableta	*a tablet*
la capsula	*a capsule*
la pastilla	*a pill*
el antibiótico	*an antibiotic*
las proteínas	*proteins*
las vitaminas	*vitamins*

El paciente necesita tomar un descongestionante al acostarse.
The patient needs to take decongestants at bed time.

al acostarse	*at bedtime*
al levantarse	*when the patient gets up*
cada *cuatro* horas	*every four hours*
antes de cada comida	*before each meal*
después de cada comida	*after each meal*
entre comidas	*between meals*
con las comidas	*with meals*
en ayunas	*first thing in the morning/ before eating anything*

¿Es usted alérgico al polen?   *Are you allergic to pollen?*
Si, soy alérgico al polen.   *Yes, I'm allergic to pollen.*

El paciente es alérgico...   *The patient is allergic to ...*

al polen	*pollen*
a los antibióticos	*antibiotics*
al latex	*latex*
a la sulfa	*sulfa*
a los barbitúricos	*barbiturates*
a los analgésicos	*analgesics*
a la inyección contra el tetano	*the tetanus shot*
a las picaduras de insectos	*insect bites*
a los descongestionantes	*decongestants*
a los perfumes y cosméticos	*perfume and cosmetics*

The verb "ser" describes permanent conditions.

El paciente es...   *The patient is...*

asmático	*asthmatic*
delgado	*thin*
alérgico a la sulfa	*allergic to sulfa*
alérgico a la penicilina	*allergic to penicillin*

The verb "estar" describes temporary conditions.

El paciente está...   *The patient is...*

    delgado   *(looks) thin*

    pálido   *pale*

    enfermo   *sick*

    resfriado   *has a cold*

    gordo   *fat*

    estreñido   *constipated*

    aventado/hinchado   *bloated*

    anémico   *anemic*

Práctica

1. Find 10 cognates in the dialogs and list them below.

   a. _____

   b. _____

   c. _____

   d. _____

   e. _____

   f. _____

   g. _____

   h. _____

   i. _____

   j. _____

2. Saber or conocer? Complete the following sentences with the verb Saber or Conocer.

   a. El doctor _____ al paciente.

   b. La paciente _____ que esta embarazada.

   c. La recepcionista _____ el número de teléfono

   del paciente.

   d. El doctor _____ los síntomas del paciente.

   e. Los pacientes _____ al doctor y a la enfermera.

3. Complete the following sentences with the verb *IR*.

    a. Yo _____ a recetar la medicina.

    b. Nosotros _____ a vacunar al niño.

    c. La enfermera _____ a recetar vitaminas.

    d. Ellos _____ a regresar mañana.

    e. El doctor _____ a recetar Kaopectate para la diarrea.

4. Complete the following sentences with the verb *Ser* or *Estar*.

    a. El paciente _____ asmático.

    b. El paciente _____ gordo.

    c. Nosotros _____ anémicos.

    d. Los pacientes _____ alérgicos a la penicilina.

    e. Yo _____ aventado y estreñido.

    f. El paciente _____ estreñido.

    g. El niño _____ enfermo.

5. Complete the following sentences with the expressions "siempre, a veces, nunca or alguien." Use each expression once.

    a. _____ como vegetales.

    b. _____ hay muchos pacientes en la sala de emergencia.

c. ¿Hay _____aquí? No hay nadie.

d. _____estoy contento/a.

6. Match the Spanish phrases with the English translation.

   a. Tiene tos.   _____He has a cold.

   b. Frota sus oídos.   _____He has pus.

   c. Tiene catarro.   _____He rubs his ears.

   d. Tiene sangre en el oído.   _____He has fever.

   e. Tiene infección en los oídos.   _____He has a cough.

   f. Tiene pus.   _____He has an ear infection.

   g. Tiene fiebre.   _____He has blood in his ear.

7. Match the following Spanish phrases with their corresponding English phrases.

   a. el tétano   _____diphtheria

   b. el sarampión   _____whooping cough

   c. la tos ferina   _____rubella

   d. la difteria   _____mumps

   e. la rubeola   _____tetanus

   f. las paperas   _____measles

8. Answer the following questions.

   a. ¿Cómo está el niño?

   b. ¿El niño tiene fiebre?

c. ¿Él tiene dolor en el oído?

d. ¿El paciente es alérgico a los antibióticos?

e. ¿Él es alérgico al latex?

f. ¿El paciente es asmático?

g. ¿Está estreñido/a el paciente?

h. ¿Él toma vitaminas?

i. ¿Su hijo necesita las vacunas?

j. ¿Su hijo tiene tos?

k. ¿Él come bien?

9. What would you say in the following situations?

a. You are Mrs. Perez. Tell the doctor that your son is sick. He is asthmatic and he is eating very little.

b. You are the doctor. Ask the patient what her symptoms are.

c. Tell the patient that you are going to vaccinate him/her against whooping cough.

d. Tell the patient that you will do a tuberculin test.

e. Tell the mother of the patient that you will vaccinate the child against measles.

f.   Ask the doctor what the child needs.

g.   Prescribe the proper medication for an ear infection.

h.   Prescribe the proper medication for diarrhea.

i.   Prescribe the proper medication for an irritated buttock.

j.   Tell the patient what to do for dehydration.

k.   Tell the patient to take the medicine at bedtime.

l.   Tell the patient to take the capsule between meals.

m.   Tell the mother to give the child children's Tylenol every four hours.

n.   Tell the patient to take vitamins and proteins every day.

o.   Ask the patient if he is allergic to analgesics.

10. Translate the following paragraph.

Carlitos está enfermo. El tiene la vacuna contra la difteria, el tétano y la tos ferina. Carlitos también tiene la vacuna oral contra la polio. Carlitos siente comezón por todo el cuerpo y tiene fiebre. Carlitos tiene los síntomas de la varicela, una enfermedad común en los niños.

Cultural Notes

Hispanics and alternative medicine

Patients usually want to find a natural remedy before using medicine the doctor prescribes. The consultation starts with 'la abuela' (grandmother). If she does not bring relief, Hispanics can visit "el yerbero" (herbalist), "el sobador" (massage therapist), "la partera" (midwife) or "el curandero" (healer). If the problem persists then they are ready to visit a doctor. In addition to what the doctor prescribes, they might include folk, herbal medicine, medicine obtained from a friend, prayer, and faith in God.

APPENDICES

Appendix 1

Las partes de la cabeza

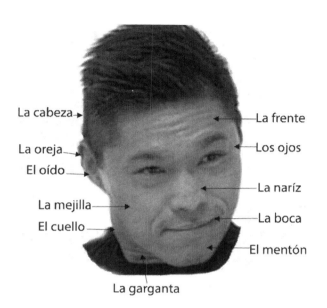

La cabeza → | ← La frente
La oreja → | Los ojos
El oído → |
La mejilla → | La naríz
El cuello → | La boca
| El mentón
La garganta

la cara	*face*
la cabeza	*head*
la oreja	*ear*
el oído	*inner ear*
la mejilla	*cheek*
el cuello	*neck*
la garganta	*throat*
la frente	*forehead*
los ojos	*eyes*
la nariz	*nose*
la boca	*mouth*
el mentón	*chin*

Appendix 2

Las partes del brazo

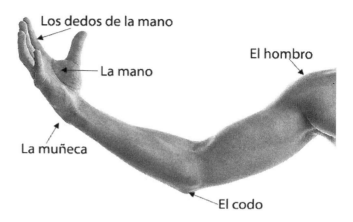

el hombro	*shoulder*
el brazo	*arm*
el codo	*elbow*
la mano	*hand*
los dedos de la mano	*fingers*
la muñeca	wrist

El pie

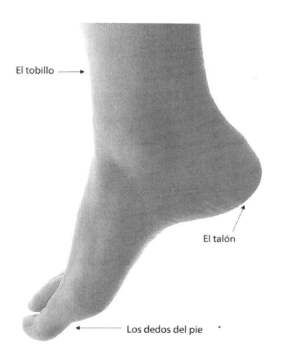

El tobillo ────▶

El talón

◀──── Los dedos del pie

el tobillo	*ankle*
los dedos del pie	toes
el talón	heel

Appendix 4

El cuerpo del hombre

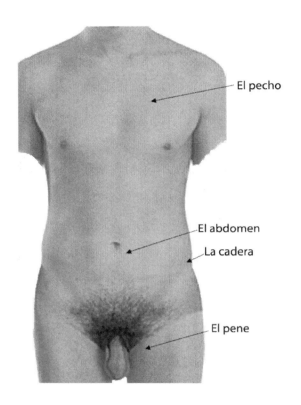

el pecho	*chest*
la cadera	*hip*
el abdomen	*abdomen*
el pene	*penis*

El cuerpo de la mujer

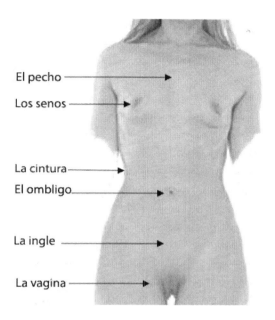

El pecho

Los senos

La cintura

El ombligo

La ingle

La vagina

el pecho	*chest*
los senos	*breasts*
el ombligo	*navel*
la ingle	*groin*
la vagina	*vagina*

Appendix 6
El cuerpo humano

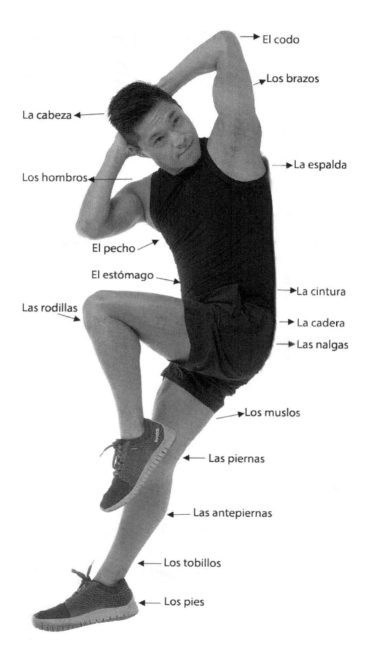

- El codo
- Los brazos
- La cabeza
- La espalda
- Los hombros
- El pecho
- El estómago
- La cintura
- La cadera
- Las nalgas
- Las rodillas
- Los muslos
- Las piernas
- Las antepiernas
- Los tobillos
- Los pies

las ante piernas	calf	**las manos**	hands
los brazos	arms	**los muslos**	thighs
la cabeza	head	**las nalgas**	buttocks
la cadera	hip	**el pecho**	chest
la cintura	waist	**las piernas**	legs
el codo	elbow	**los pies**	feet
el estómago	stomach	**las rodillas**	knees
la espalda	back	**los tobillos**	ankles
los hombros	shoulders		

Appendix 7

Órganos internos

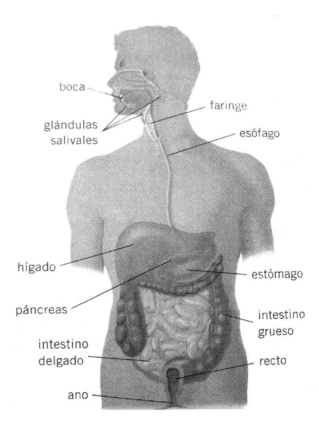

obca	*mouth*
glándulas salivales	*salivary glands*
faringe	*pharynx*
esófago	*esophagus*
hígado	*liver*
estómago	*stomach*
pancreas	*pancreas*
intestino Delgado	*small intestine*
intestino grueso	*large intestine*
recto	*rectum*
ano	*anus*

El esqueleto

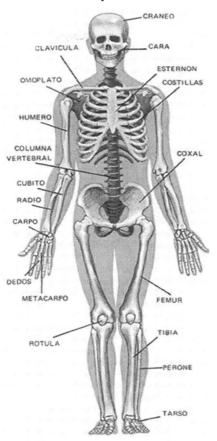

clavícula	*clavicle*	**craneo**	*skull*
omoplato	*shoulder blade*	**cara**	*face*
humero	*humerus*	**esternon**	*sternum*
columna vertebral	*spine*	**costillas**	*ribs*
cubito	*ulna*	**coxal**	*coxal*
radio	*radius*	**femur**	*femur*
carpo	*carpal*	**tibia**	*tibia*
dedos	*fingers*	**peroné**	*fibula*
metacarpo	*metacarpus*	**tarso**	*tarsus*
rotula	*kneecap*		

Appendix 9   Dialogs translation

LESSON 1   Requesting basic information from the patient.

Dialog 1

Receptionist fills out a form

Receptionist:	Good morning (Mrs.)
Patient:	Good morning (Miss)
Receptionist:	Name and last name?
Patient:	Ana Camacho.
Receptionist:	Address?
Patient:	18 Salem Street, Lynn MA.
Receptionist:	Telephone number?
Patient:	781-524-2764.
Receptionist:	Date of birth?
Patient:	December 24th, 1977.
Receptionist:	Where are you from?
Patient:	I'm from Lynn.
Receptionist:	Are you single or married?
Patient:	I'm married.

Dialog 2

Receptionist:	Good morning. Come in and have a seat, please. How can I help you?
Patient:	Good morning. I need to speak with the nurse.
Receptionist:	Very well.
Patient:	Thank you.
Receptionist:	You're welcome.

Dialog 3

Doctor:	Good evening Mrs. Vega. I'm Dr. Smith. How are you feeling?
Patient:	Not very well, doctor.
Doctor:	I'm sorry.

Dialog 4

Doctor:	Good afternoon, Mrs. Loza.
Patient:	Good afternoon, doctor.
Doctor:	How are you?
Patient:	Awful.
Doctor:	I'm sorry! I only speak a little bit of Spanish. I need to call an interpreter.

LESSON 2   A physical exam. Which body parts hurts? How much do they hurt?

Dialog 1

Receptionist:	Good morning. How can I help you?
Patient:	Good morning. I have a physical examination with Dr. Polo.
Receptionist:	Very well. Name and last name, please?
Patient:	I'm Elena Gómez.
Receptionist:	Do you have your medical insurance card? I need a photocopy.
Patient:	Here it is.
Receptionist:	You need to fill out the form.

Dialog 2

Receptionist:	Good afternoon. How can I help you?
Patient:	Good afternoon. I have an appointment with Dr. Ramos.
Receptionist:	Name and last name, please?
Patient:	Elena Gómez.
Receptionist:	I need your medical insurance card.
Patient:	I do not have medical insurance.
Receptionist:	Will you pay the bill?
Patient:	Yes, I (will) pay the bill.

Dialog 3

Doctor:	You have a general checkup today. How are you feeling, Mrs. Vera?
Patient:	Very well, doctor.
Doctor:	You need a pap smear and a mammogram. You also need a blood and urine test. Do you still have headaches?
Patient:	Yes. I have migraines.
Doctor:	Here is the prescription for the migraines.
Patient:	Thank you!

Dialog 4

Doctor:	How are you feeling, Mrs. Vargas?
Patient:	I have headaches, doctor.
Doctor:	Do your eyes hurt?
Patient:	Yes, my eyes hurt a lot.
Doctor:	Does your neck hurt?
Patient:	No, my neck does not hurt.
Doctor:	Do you hear noise in your ears?
Patient:	Yes doctor, I hear noise in my ears.
Doctor:	Do you have difficulty breathing?
Patient:	No, I do not have difficulty breathing.
Doctor:	Do you have a cough?
Patient:	I don't have a cough.

LESSON 3 An appointment with the primary care physician

Dialog 1

Nurse:	Mr. Ortiz. I speak Spanish. We do not need an interpreter. How much do you weigh?
Patient:	I weigh 180 pounds.
Nurse:	How tall are you?
Patient:	I'm five feet, seven inches.
Nurse:	How are you feeling?
Patient:	Not very well.

Dialog 2

Doctor:	Where does it hurt?
Patient:	My stomach hurts.
Doctor:	Does it hurt a lot or a little?
Patient:	It hurts a lot.
Doctor:	From 1 to 10, how much does it hurt?
Patient:	8.
Doctor:	Can you describe the pain?
Patient:	The pain is sharp.
Doctor:	Do you take any medicine?
Patient:	I take medicine for diabetes.

Dialog 3

Doctor:	Do you smoke?
Patient:	Yes, I smoke a little.
Doctor:	Do you cough a lot?
Patient:	Yes, I cough a lot.
Doctor:	Do you vomit?
Patient:	Yes, I vomit.
Doctor:	Do you vomit blood?
Patient:	Yes. I vomit blood sometimes.
Doctor:	Where does it hurt?
Patient:	My back and my throat hurt.
Doctor:	Is the pain strong?
Patient:	The pain is strong on my back.
Doctor:	You need some tests.

Dialog 4   *A patient with high blood pressure.*

Doctor:	How are you, Mr. Pérez?
Patient:	I'm tired, I have a headache, and I'm also dizzy.
Doctor:	Since when do you have a headache?
Patient:	A week, doctor.
Doctor:	Where does it hurt?
Patient:	Here, on my forehead.
Doctor:	Do you have swollen ankles?
Patient:	Yes, my ankles are swollen in the evenings.
Doctor:	Do you get nose bleeds?
Patient:	Yes, a little.

Doctor:	Do you eat salty foods? Do you drink alcoholic beverages?
Patient:	Yes, I like salt and I drink wine.
Doctor:	Your medical history shows high blood pressure. You need a prescription. I advise you to talk with a nutritionist to change your diet.

LESSON 4   Talking with the dietitian/nutritionist. A healthy diet.

At the hospital

Dialog 1   The dietitian/nutritionist

Dietitian:	Good morning, Miss Vera. How are you?
Patient	Well, thank you.
Dietitian:	For breakfast we have cereal with milk and yogurt.
Patient	Can I have eggs and toast for breakfast?
Dietitian:	It is important to avoid greasy foods and have a balanced diet. What do you generally drink?
Patient	I like to drink coffee. I drink decaffeinated coffee.
Dietitian:	I advise you to drink low fat milk or fruit smoothies.

Dialog 2

Dietitian:	What would you like for lunch?
Patient	I am not hungry.
Dietitian:	It is important to eat something. I advise you to eat steamed rice with chicken and to drink water.
Patient:	I do not like water.

Dialog 3

Dietitian:	Mr. Pérez, your son should avoid sugar and greasy foods because he is overweight and malnourished.
Sr. Pérez:	What should I do?
Dietitian:	It is important to eat small portions, avoid greasy foods, and sodas.
Sr. Pérez:	What can he eat?

Dietitian: Your son can eat vegetables and fruits. Here is a list of healthy foods.

Dialog 4

Patient: I need to lose weight.
Dietitian: What do you generally eat?
Patient: I generally eat sweets, cakes, and drink soda.
Dietitian: To avoid heart problems and diabetes, you should follow a strict diet.
Patient: It is too difficult!
Dietitian: Yes, but it is important to lose weight. Here is a list of healthy foods for you. It is important to count your calorie intake and exercise.

LESSON 5   An appointment with the gynecologist.

Dialog 1   *The gynecologist (female doctor) and the pregnant patient.*

Doctor: Good Morning, Mrs. Vera. How are you?
Mrs. Vera: Not very well doctor.
Doctor: What symptoms do you have?
Mrs. Vera: I have not had my period since February.
Doctor: Is your period regular or irregular?
Mrs. Vera: It is regular, doctor.
Doctor: Okay. Are you dizzy? Are you nauseous? Are you tired?
Mrs. Vera: Yes, I'm dizzy and nauseous. I'm always tired.
Doctor: Are you vomiting?
Mrs. Vera: I vomit in the mornings.
Doctor: Are your breasts swollen or hard?
Mrs. Vera: My breasts are swollen and also hard.
Doctor: Do you urinate frequently?
Mrs. Vera: Yes, I urinate frequently.
Doctor: You need a urine test, a blood test, and a vaginal exam.

Dialog 2

Doctor:	How old are you, Mrs. Pérez?
Mrs. Pérez:	I'm 45 years old, doctor.
Doctor:	Congratulations! You are pregnant. We have to be careful because this is a high risk pregnancy.
Mrs. Pérez:	What should I do, doctor?
Doctor:	You have to follow my instructions.

Dialog 3

Doctor:	Mrs. Vera, congratulations! You are pregnant.
Mrs. Vera:	Thank you, doctor.
Doctor:	Do you smoke?
Mrs. Vera:	Yes, I smoke a pack daily.
Doctor:	You have to stop smoking because it is bad for the baby and for you too.
Mrs. Vera:	Very well, doctor.
Doctor:	Do you drink alcoholic beverages?
Mrs. Vera:	I drink a little.
Doctor:	You should avoid alcoholic beverages. You have to rest and avoid heavy work. You need to drink lots of liquids but avoid caffeine, soda, and drugs in general.
Mrs. Vera:	Do I need a diet?
Doctor:	Yes, if you are hungry you should eat lots of fruits and vegetables.
Mrs. Vera:	Very well, doctor.
Doctor:	Mrs. Vera, you need to return next month.

Dialog 4

Doctor:	Mrs. Poma, the nurse is bringing your medical file in a moment.
Mrs. Poma:	Thank you, doctor.
Doctor:	Are you coming to get the blood test tomorrow?
Mrs. Poma:	Yes, I am coming tomorrow.

The next day

Doctor:	The tests came back negative, Mrs. Poma. You are not pregnant.

Dialog 5

Family Planning Center. The female doctor talks to a group of young women.

Doctor:	To avoid pregnancy you need to take contraceptive pills. There are also other methods.
Young girl:	What are the other methods to avoid pregnancy?
Doctor:	The IDU (Intrauterine device), a monthly shot, condoms, and abstinence. The pills are more effective. The condoms are necessary to avoid diseases. Abortion is an option in case of unwanted pregnancy.

LESSON 6 An appointment with the pediatrician. Sicknesses, remedies, and vaccines. The pediatrician and the child's parents

Dialog 1

Pediatrician:	How is Juanito today?
Mrs. Pérez:	Juanito is sick, doctor.
Pediatrician:	What are his symptoms?
Mrs. Pérez:	He rubs his ears a lot.
Pediatrician:	Does the child have a fever?
Mrs. Pérez:	Yes, he has a fever of 103 and he also has a cold.
Pediatrician:	Is he coughing?
Mrs. Pérez:	Yes, doctor. He has a cough.
Pediatrician:	I'm going to examine Juanito.

Later

Pediatrician:	Juanito has an ear infection. There is pus and blood in his left ear. I'll prescribe an antibiotic and a decongestant. Is the child allergic to antibiotics or decongestants?
Mrs. Perez:	No, doctor.

Dialog 2

Mrs. Pérez:	My son has a cold and has asthma, doctor.
Pediatrician:	How old is the child?
Mrs. Pérez:	He is two years old.
Pediatrician:	The child is very thin, Mrs. Perez. He only weighs 20 pounds.
Mrs. Pérez:	Yes, my son eats very little and is always constipated and bloated.
Pediatrician:	He is very pale. The child might be anemic. He needs a blood test. You need to take the child to the lab before he eats anything. You should also talk to the nutritionist.

Dialog 3

Mrs. Vera:	What does my daughter need, doctor?
Pediatrician:	She needs to take children's Tylenol every four hours.

Dialog 4

Nurse:	Mrs. Vera, your son needs to be vaccinated against tetanus, whooping cough, and diphtheria.
Mrs. Vera:	Very well.
Nurse:	We are also going to do a tuberculosis test (TB test) next time.

Appendix 10　　Regular Verbs

abrir	*To open*
aprender	*To learn*
bailar	*To dance*
beber	*To drink*
cambiar	*To change*
cancelar	*To cancel*
cantar	*To sing*
cenar	*To have dinner*
cortar	*To cut*
creer	*To believe*
comprar	*To buy*
correr	*To run*
comer	*To eat*
dañar	*To hurt*
dar	*To give*
deber	*Should/must*
desayunar	*To have breakfast*
descansar	*To rest*

desear	*To wish*
dibujar	*To draw*
escribir	*To write*
esperar	*To wait*
estudiar	*To study*
entrar	*To enter*
enviar	*To send*
examinar	*To examine*
expectora	*To spit out*
explicar	*To explain*
firmar	*to sign*
fumar	*To smoke*
hablar	*To talk*
intentar	*To try*
leer	*To read*
limpiar	*To clean*
llamar	*To call*
llenar	*To fill out*
mirar	*To watch*
medir	*To measure*
mirar	*To look at*
necesitar	*To need*

organizar	*To organize*
olvidar	*To forget*
orinar	*To urinate*
pagar	*To pay*
peinar	*To comb*
pesar	*To weight*
preocuparse	*To worry*
preguntar	*To ask*
prestar	*To borrow*
responder	*To reply*
regresar	*To return*
sangrar	*To bleed*
toser	*To cough*
terminar	*To finish*
tomar	*To take, drink*
tener	*to have*
trabajar	*To work*
utilizar/usar	*To wear, to use*
vender	*To sell*
viajar	*To travel*
vivir	*To live*
vomitar	*To vomit*

Conjugation of Regular verbs ending in AR, ER and IR.

Examples:

hablar	comer	vivir
hab**lo**	com**o**	viv**o**
hab**las**	com**es**	viv**es**
hab**la**	com**e**	viv**e**
hab**lamos**	com**emos**	viv**imos**
hab**lais**	com**eis**	viv**isteis**
hab**lan**	com**en**	viv**en**

Appendix 11 Conjugation of regular verbs

Regular AR verbs

Bajar *to go down*

Yo bajo
Tú bajas
Usted baja
El baja
Ella baja
Nosotros bajamos
Ustedes bajan
Ellos bajan
Ellas bajan

Descansar *to rest*

Yo descanso
Tú descansas
Usted descansa
El descansa
Ella descansa
Nosotros descansamos
Ustedes descansan
Ellos descansan
Ellas descansan

Evitar *to avoid*

Yo evito
Tú evitas
Usted evita
El evita
Ella evita
Nosotros evitamos
Ustedes evitan
Ellos evitan
Ellas evitan

Comprar *to buy*

Yo compro
Tú compras
Usted compra
El compra
Ella compra
Nosotros compramos
Ustedes compran
Ellos compran
Ellas compran

Examinar *to examine*

Yo examino
Tú examinas
Usted examina
El examina
Ella examina
Nosotros examinamos
Ustedes examinan
Ellos examinan
Ellas examinan

Fumar *to smoke*

Yo fumo
Tú fumas
Usted fuma
El fuma
Ella fuma
Nosotros fumamos
Ustedes fuman
Ellos fuman
Ellas fuman

Chequear *to check*

Yo chequeo
Tú chequeas
Usted chequea
El chequea
Ella chequea
Nosotros chequeamos
Ustedes chequean
Ellos chequean
Ellas chequean

Estudiar *to study*

Yo estudio
Tú estudias
Usted estudia
El estudia
Ella estudia
Nosotros estudiamos
Ustedes estudian
Ellos estudian
Ellas estudian

Hablar *to speak*

Yo hablo
Tú hablas
Usted habla
El habla
Ella habla
Nosotros hablamos
Ustedes hablan
Ellos hablan
Ellas hablan

Desayunar *to have breakfast*

Yo desayuno
Tú desayunas
Usted desayuna
El desayuna
Ella desayuna
Nosotros desayunamos
Ustedes desayunan
Ellos desayunan
Ellas desayunan

Entrar *to enter*

Yo entro
Tú entras
Usted entra
El entra
Ella entra
Nosotros entramos
Ustedes entran
Ellos entran
Ellas entran

Llamar *to call*

Yo llamo
Tú llamas
Usted llama
El llama
Ella llama
Nosotros llamamos
Ustedes llaman
Ellos llaman
Ellas llaman

Desear *to want/to wish*

Yo deseo
Tú deseas
Usted desea
El desea
Ella desea
Nosotros deseamos
Ustedes desean
Ellos desean
Ellas desean

Esperar *to wait for*

Yo espero
Tú esperas
Usted espera
El espera
Ella espera
Nosotros esperamos
Ustedes esperan
Ellos esperan
Ellas esperan

Llenar *to fill out*

Yo lleno
Tú llenas
Usted llena
El llena
Ella llena
Nosotros llenamos
Ustedes llenan
Ellos llenan
Ellas llenan

Llegar *to arrive*

Yo llego
Tú llegas
Usted llega
El llega
Ella llega
Nosotros llegamos
Ustedes llegan
Ellos llegan
Ellas llegan

Orinar *to urinate*

Yo orino
Tú orinas
Usted orina
El orina
Ella orina
Nosotros orinamos
Ustedes orinan
Ellos orinan
Ellas orinan

Revisar *to check*

Yo reviso
Tú revisas
Usted revisa
El revisa
Ella revisa
Nosotros revisamos
Ustedes revisan
Ellos revisan
Ellas revisan

Llevar *to take* (someone or something)	**Pagar** *to pay*	**Tomar** *to take/to drink*
Yo llevo	Yo pago	Yo tomo
Tú llevas	Tú pagas	Tú tomas
Usted lleva	Usted paga	Usted toma
El lleva	El paga	El toma
Ella lleva	Ella paga	Ella toma
Nosotros llevamos	Nosotros pagamos	Nosotros tomamos
Ustedes llevan	Ustedes pagan	Ustedes toman
Ellos llevan	Ellos pagan	Ellos toman
Ellas llevan	Ellas pagan	Ellas toman

Limpiar *to clean*	**Pesar** *to weigh*	**Trabajar** *to work*
Yo limpio	Yo peso	Yo trabajo
Tú limpias	Tú pesas	Tú trabajas
Usted limpia	Usted pesa	Usted trabaja
El limpia	El pesa	El trabaja
Ella limpia	Ella pesa	Ella trabaja
Nosotros limpiamos	Nosotros pesamos	Nosotros trabajamos
Ustedes limpian	Ustedes pesan	Ustedes trabajan
Ellos limpian	Ellos pesan	Ellos trabajan
Ellas limpian	Ellas pesan	Ellas trabajan

Mirar *to look at*	**Recetar** *to prescribe*	**Usar** *to wear, to use*
Yo miro	Yo receto	Yo uso
Tú miras	Tú recetas	Tú usas
Usted mira	Usted receta	Usted usa
El mira	El receta	El usa
Ella mira	Ella receta	Ella usa
Nosotros miramos	Nosotros recetamos	Nosotros usamos
Ustedes miran	Ustedes recetan	Ustedes usan
Ellos miran	Ellos recetan	Ellos usan
Ellas miran	Ellas recetan	Ellas usan

Necesitar *to need*

Yo necesito
Tú necesitas
Usted necesita
El necesita
Ella necesita
Nosotros necesitamos
Ustedes necesitan
Ellos necesitan
Ellas necesitan

Viajar *to travel*

Yo viajo
Tú viajas
Usted viaja
El viaja
Ella viaja
Nosotros viajamos
Ustedes viajan
Ellos viajan
Ellas viajan

Visitar *to visit*

Yo visito
Tú visitas
Usted visita
El visita
Ella visita
Nosotros visitamos
Ustedes visitan
Ellos visitan
Ellas visitan

Regresar *to return*

Yo regreso
Tú regresas
Usted regresa
El regresa
Ella regresa
Nosotros regresamos
Ustedes regresan
Ellos regresan
Ellas regresan

Vomitar *to throw up*

Yo vomito
Tú vomitas
Usted vomita
El vomita
Ella vomita
Nosotros vomitamos
Ustedes vomitan
Ellos vomitan
Ellas vomitan

Vacunar *to vaccinate*

Yo vacuno
Tú vacunas
Usted vacuna
El vacuna
Ella vacuna
Nosotros vacunamos
Ustedes vacunan
Ellos vacunan
Ellas vacunan

Regular verbs - Verbos Regulares -ER

Aprender *to learn*

Yo aprendo
Tú aprendes
Usted aprende
El aprende
Ella aprende
Nosotros aprendemos
Ustedes aprenden
Ellos aprenden
Ellas aprenden

Beber *to drink*

Yo bebo
Tú bebes
Usted bebe
El bebe
Ella bebe
Nosotros bebemos
Ustedes beben
Ellos beben
Ellas beben

Comer *to eat*

Yo como
Tú comes
Usted come
El come
Ella come
Nosotros comemos
Ustedes comen
Ellos comen
Ellas comen

Creer *to think*

Yo creo
Tú crees
Usted cree
El cree
Ella cree
Nosotros creemos
Ustedes creen
Ellos creen
Ellas creen

Deber *must, should*

Yo debo
Tú debes
Usted debe
El debe
Ella debe
Nosotros debemos
Ustedes deben
Ellos deben
Ellas deben

Leer *to read*

Yo leo
Tú lees
Usted lee
El lee
Ella lee
Nosotros leemos
Ustedes leen
Ellos leen
Ellas leen

Toser *to cough*

Yo toso
Tú toses
Usted tose
El tose
Ella tose
Nosotros tosemos
Ustedes tosen
Ellos tosen
Ellas tosen

Ver *to see*

Yo veo
Tú ves
Usted ve
El ve
Ella ve
Nosotros vemos
Ustedes ven
Ellos ven
Ellas ven

Regular verbs - Verbos Regulares -IR

Abrir *to open*

Yo abro
Tú abres
Usted abre
El abre
Ella abre
Nosotros abrimos
Ustedes abren
Ellos abren
Ellas abren

Cubrir *to cover*

Yo cubro
Tú cubres
Usted cubre
El cubre
Ella cubre
Nosotros cubrimos
Ustedes cubren
Ellos cubren
Ellas cubren

Decidir *to decide*

Yo decido
Tú decides
Usted decide
El decide
Ella decide
Nosotros decidimos
Ustedes deciden
Ellos deciden
Ellas deciden

Escribir *to write*

Yo escribo
Tú escribes
Usted escribe
El escribe
Ella escribe
Nosotros escribimos
Ustedes escriben
Ellos escriben
Ellas escriben

Recibir *to receive*

Yo recibo
Tú recibes
Usted recibe
El recibe
Ella recibe
Nosotros recibimos
Ustedes reciben
Ellos reciben
Ellas reciben

Sufrir *to suffer*

Yo sufro
Tú sufres
Usted sufre
El sufre
Ella sufre
Nosotros sufrimos
Ustedes sufren
Ellos sufren
Ellas sufren

Vivir *to live*

Yo vivo
Tú vives
Usted vive
El vive
Ella vive
Nosotros vivimos
Ustedes viven
Ellos viven
Ellas viven

Appendix 12   Example of Irregular verbs

caber	To fit
conducir	To drive
conocer	To know
estar	To be
hacer	To do
herir	To hurt
dar	To give
hacer	To make/do
ir	To go
medir	To measure
oír	To hear
poner	To put
saber	To know
ser	To be
salir	To leave
tener	To have
traer	To bring
traducir	To translate
venir	To come
ver	To see

Verb to be

Ser	Estar	
soy	estoy	I'm
eres	estás	You are
es	está	He is, she is, you are
somos	estamos	We are
sois	estais	You are informal plural Spain
son	están	They are, you all are

Verbs that are irregular in the YO form.

tener	tengo
venir	vengo
ir	voy
dar	doy
estar	estoy
salir	salgo
hacer	hago
poner	pongo
traer	traigo
conducir	conduzco
traducir	traduzco
conocer	conozco
caber	quepo
ver	veo
saber	sé

Verbo Gustar		Verbo Doler	
Me gusta/n	Nos gusta/n	Me duele/n	Nos duele/n
Te gusta/n	Os gusta/n	Te duele/n	Os duele/n
Le gusta/n	Les gusta/n	Le duele/n	Les duele/n

Appendix 13   Stem-changing verbs

e > ie

cerrar	To close/shut
comenzar	To start, to begin
despertar	To wake up
empezar	To begin, to start
entender	To understand
preferir	To prefer
pensar	To think
perder	To lose
querer	To want
sentir	To feel

o > ue

almorzar	To have lunch
contar	To count
costar	To cost
dormir	To sleep
encontrar	To find
jugar	To play
llover	To rain
mostrar	To show
poder	To be able to/can
recordar	To remember
volver	To return

e > i

conseguir	To get
decir	To tell, to say
pedir	To ask for
servir	To serve
seguir	To follow
vestir	To wear, to dress

Conjugation of Stem-changing verbs

The root changes except the "nosotros and vosotros" form.

Yo com<u>ie</u>nzo	Nosotros comenzamos
Tú com<u>ie</u>nzas	Vosotros comenzáis
El ⎤	Ellos ⎤
ella ⎬ com<u>ie</u>nza	ellas ⎬ com<u>ie</u>nzan
Ud. ⎦	Uds. ⎦

todos los días	*everyday*
siempre	*always*
nunca	*never*
a veces	*sometimes*
una vez al mes	*once a month*
una vez al año	*once a year*
por la mañana	*in the morning*
por la tarde	*in the afternoon*
por la noche	*in the evening*

Appendix 15

Affirmative and Negative Expressions

Affirmative Expressions		Negative Expressions	
siempre	*always*	nunca	*never*
a veces	*sometimes*	jamás	*never*
algo	*something,*	nada	*nothing*
alguien	*someone*	nadie	*nobody, no one*
algún	*anything*	ningún	*none*
alguno/a,	*some, any*	ninguno/a,	*none*
algunos/as	*some, any*	ningunos/as	

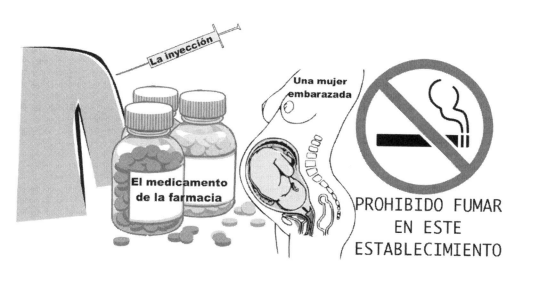

La inyección

Una mujer embarazada

El medicamento de la farmacia

PROHIBIDO FUMAR EN ESTE ESTABLECIMIENTO

Image Sources

Lesson 1
http://commons.wikimedia.org/wiki/File:Dr._Phillips_Hospital_Pat_Reg
_Desk.jpg
http://blogs.strat-cons.com/?p=910

Lesson 2
http://www.freestockphotos.biz/stockphoto/15413

Lesson 3

http://en.wikipedia.org/wiki/Physical_examination#/media/File:Elderly
_vietnamese_man_gets_examined.jpg

Lesson 4
https://upload.wikimedia.org/wikipedia/commons/e/e9/Soy-whey-
protein-diet.jpg

Lesson 5
http://en.wikipedia.org/wiki/Maternal_physiological_changes_in_pregn
ancy#/media/File:Swanger_vrou2.jpg

Lesson 6
http://upload.wikimedia.org/wikipedia/commons/c/c9/An_Indian_phys
ician_examines_boy_on_Gunungsitoli.jpg

Appendix

http://skat.ihmc.us/rid=1MCNV9TNZ-53Q225-25TF/
http://aloim.org/cuerpo-humano-para-colorear-con-sus-partes/
https://pixabay.com/en/abdominal-abs-exercise-body-1203881/

48411808R00096

Made in the USA
Columbia, SC
09 January 2019